MW00638124

WOMAN
OF
ROYALTY

Rule from a Place of Authority

BRIANA WHITESIDE

Limits of Liability and Disclaimer of Warranty

The author and publisher shall not be liable for your misuse of this material. This book is strictly for informational and educational purposes. The purpose of this book is to educate and entertain. The author and/or publisher do not guarantee that anyone following these techniques, suggestions, tips, ideas, or strategies will become successful. The author and/or publisher shall have neither liability nor responsibility to anyone with respect to any loss or damage caused, or alleged to be caused, directly or indirectly by the information contained in this book.

Views expressed in this publication do not necessarily reflect the views of the publisher.

Printed in the United States of America

Cover Design: Justin Smith
Editing: Raven Douglas

ISBN: 978-1-948270-24-3
Keen Vision Publishing, LLC
www.keen-vision.com

For you, the reader.
May you forever live as the queen God created
you to be.

CONTENTS

FOREWORD

"For as he thinks in his heart, so is he [in behavior—one who manipulates]. He says to you, "Eat and drink," Yet his heart is not with you [but it is begrudging the cost]."

Proverbs 23:7

Who do you believe you are? What thoughts have crept into your heart? Did you know you are highly thought of? Are you aware that you are a precious jewel? Did you know that you are beautiful? Did you know that you are one of God's greatest creations?

Have you allowed life to define who you are? Have you allowed society's oppression to define you? Have you allowed the voids in your life to shape you? Have those voids caused you to run away from who you truly are? Was it abuse? Has it been those secrets that you hide in shame? What has caused you to run from reality?

As I ponder these questions, I can't help but remember the times when I saw the anguish on your face because you felt you didn't measure up. I could not help but gasp for air because my heart was broken when someone broke yours. I remember when I wanted to hold you and take away your pain only to realize that I could not. I would sit in silence and pray that the Lord would reveal to you who you truly are. My prayer has been that you would come into the knowledge of how important you are. Not to me, but to this world. Did you know that creation moans and groans for the manifestation of the sons of God (Romans 8:9)?

As your parent, watching you go through life with its twists and turns, I often wonder what I could have done differently. I should have explained things differently. Maybe you would have made different choices. Not different, but better. Maybe I should have changed locations. What if I only worked one job and poured into you, would it have kept you from making the same mistakes over and over? So many times I wonder how I could have done things differently. I have asked myself if I could have done more to protect you. I can't explain how precious you are to me.

Even with all those questions, I have come to realize that there was nothing more I could have done because you had an appointment with destiny. It was time for your steps to be ordered by God. In essence, I had to decrease in your life so that you would find the abundance of life. I had to stand by, watching, and interceding while you fully submitted yourself to the Lord. There were moments when I wanted to swoop in like supermom and save the day. Unfortunately, this would have only delayed your process and caused more pain and anguish.

As I look at the woman you have become, I cannot help but say, "This is the Lord's doing and it is marvelous in my eyes."

(Psalm 118:23). Daughter, when God created you, he said, "IT IS GOOD!"

Written by Latice Woodard

Introduction

The Bible neither identifies every woman by name, nor titles many books after them. Nodding to the latter, there are only two books in the Bible dedicated to women, which are Ruth and Esther, located in the Old Testament. On the one hand, much has been written and taught about Ruth and her unusual level of faith to stand by her mother-in-law long after the death of her husband. Indeed, Ruth's journey is one that inspires the reader to progress in the face of despair and in the end she marries Boaz. Perhaps you may have heard a woman say that she's waiting for God to send her Boaz. What she means is that she is waiting for God to send her a husband who will cover her and provide for her honorably, the way that Boaz did for Ruth. If you're interested in her personal journey and the love story, then you should definitely read the book of Ruth in order to gain a deeper understanding of their lives.

On the other hand, Queen Esther's story is one that tells of a young girls' journey from obscurity to becoming a Queen in the palace. Esther's coming of age story is very important for women on the quest to find their identity outside of secular possessions because so many times we make the error of finding our identity in the relationships that we have, the jobs we hold, and the accolades we obtain. Yet, eventually we find that those things let us down time and time again. But what if there was a way not to be left empty? What if I told you that there was a way to ensure fulfillment? Would you trust me enough to allow me show you the way? If so, I'll share one nugget with you now: the secret to finding fulfillment and ultimately your royal identity in Christ is through obedience. Yes, obedience!

Now, I must be honest and tell you that obedience is not an easy task. Contrary to popular belief, if we were more obedient to the promptings and commands of God, the world may be a better place. But because we have desires, wants, needs, and free will, many of us struggle in the place of obedience. Ultimately, obedience requires you to give up the things you want for the things you need. It demands that you not talk to that cute guy that you know will ruin your life, or it encourages you to leave a job that you believe will set you up for success. At times, it even requires that you be silent when you really want to clap back at someone for being disrespectful. Honestly, obedience is hard, but it is not impossible. Even more, being obedient means that you have self-control and are signaling to God that He can trust you with your destiny.

Sometimes I wonder if people recognize the things that we forfeit by being disobedient. Take a second and think about the possibility of your actions causing you to settle for places where you don't fit. They may be the moments where you find yourself wondering if there is more to life than this. If you can relate to the aforementioned statement, then you have picked up the right book. One of the reasons we struggle to obey God the first time is due to our inability to fully trust Him. Too often we don't trust Him to be a way maker, we don't trust Him to bring the mate He promised, and we definitely don't trust Him to heal our emotions. Unfortunately, we treat Him as if He were the individuals who once let us down, which is unfair to Him and us. Ultimately, being obedient to God is a daily decision that requires us to act purposefully in accordance to His will, and realize that the level of obedience He required of us when we first were saved is not the level He will require years later. As we move from glory to glory and from faith to faith, there will be new demands on our obedience that will challenge old systems of operation.

Stylistically, this book is written parallel to the book of Esther. Consequently, it is written in ten chapters that chronicle and correspond to Esther's life, plight, and struggles. More importantly, this book highlights exact moments where Esther made important choices to either obey God or her emotions. I draw attention to the times when she had to decide if she would believe in an invisible man or fear the King of the land.

I don't want to assume that you are acquainted with Esther, so I would like to tell you briefly about her life. Esther is a woman in the Bible who was orphaned due to the death of both parents when she was young. As a result, her cousin Mordecai cared for her until there was a decree issued to find a new Queen. Due to the insubordination of the current Queen Vashti, all of the virgins in the city were gathered to have one night in the palace in hopes of being chosen as the replacement. Theologians agree that Esther was between the ages of 13-15 when the decree was made, but as an inhabitant, she was ordered to the kingdom whether she wanted to go or not. The Bible tells us that when Esther went before the King, she found favor and eventually became the new Queen.

Interestingly though, her new positioning as Queen did not rid her of her responsibility to the Jews in their time of need. As both Jew and Queen, Esther found herself negotiating between her former designation as a Jewish woman and her new position and responsibility as Queen. More plainly, there were times when the two were in direct opposition with one another, but instead of casting one off for the other, Esther used the intersectionality of her identity to her advantage. In the end, Esther's Jewish heritage assisted in the process of becoming who she was destined to be. While she was always created to be a Queen, there were steps that were necessary to get her to the royal place. Furthermore, the steps could not have been realized without her ability to yield to the promptings of God. With this in mind, women can learn a lot from Queen Esther because her grace, poise, and attitude aided in a successful and obedient rein, though she struggled with identity.

Esther's battle with identity mirrors so many women's struggle. Personally, because I grew up in a single parent home, my perception of my life and capability were skewed. There were times that I entered into relationships that I had no business entertaining, and also found myself willfully settling for positions that I knew were beneath me. Though I knew I was settling and possibly on the road to destruction, I didn't know where to find the nearest exit. Like Esther, I too struggled with negotiating between the various forms of my identity. As a higher education scholar and Christian, there have been times in my own life that I tried to trade one for the other, which left me unfulfilled and depressed. It wasn't until I discovered that my identity as a scholar is largely informed by my spiritual journey that I had peace. And I came into this awareness through intentional obedience to God. In essence, I had to give God a hard "yes" in an area of my life that I thought would kill me, but it was the very hard "yes" that set me up to find my destiny and ultimately write this book.

Together the biblical story of Esther and my personal journey with obedience and identity braid this book. As I weave my story within the revelation of Esther's life, I hope that my transparency will allow you to inspect the areas within yourself that you may have neglected. This book is not designed in a manner that will allow you to get through it in one sitting. In fact, you may find yourself overwhelmed if you try to do so. Instead, it is my suggestion that you read the book of Esther and then work through this text as the Holy Spirit leads you. You may notice that there are rhetorical questions that I may pose to prompt awareness within you, but it is solely up to you to do the work of unpacking what applies to your life. I believe this book will bring you a level of healing in areas that you have been left scarred due to your disobedience to God. It is my prayer that through this book you will have the desire and courage to embrace your position as a Woman of Royalty. I hope that you will find the strength that will allow you to obey God at any cost. I also pray that you will be given the grace and peace to take strides in embodying your identity in Christ.

Your palace waits!

Chapter One

THE ROYAL ARENA IS SET

"I will go before you and level the mountains; I will shatter the doors of bronze and cut through the bars of iron. I will give you the treasures of darkness [the hoarded treasures] And the hidden riches of secret places, So that you may know that it is I, The Lord, the God of Israel, who calls you by your name."

Isaiah 45:2-3

W orry is a human reaction to things out of our control. When we worry we acknowledge that we've come to the end of ourselves, but more times than not, we aren't sure which way to turn. It is possible that we desperately want to make things work out, even if they are hard. But sometimes we just can't and the sense of failure that looms over our heads has the potential to haunt us long after the event is over.

If you're anything like me, then you probably wrack your brain to come up with solutions to your problems. You might try everything you know to do, but when the end result does not yield victory, you may wonder about your worthiness and capabilities. Yet, rarely, if ever, do we stop to think that sometimes we do not have things due to our inability to obey God. We don't consider that while we are begging God to fix, or turn the situation around, He is asking us to stop aggravating the circumstance.

The scripture in Isaiah highlights God's love for us, and demonstrates that God wants to take care of us if only we'd let Him. It also reveals that He will go before us to the destined place to make sure things are in order when we get there. God assures that He will do all the hard work so that we can have an easier time reaching the promise. Perhaps the most exciting part of the scripture is that He also promises us treasures and riches that have yet to be uncovered.

I believe the most important revelation about the Isaiah scripture is that God says He will give us all these things so that we will trust in Him more. The reason He wants us to trust Him is not so that we can brag to our friends, but to encourage a deeper relationship with Him unlike any we've ever had. And, through a more intimate relationship we will find our identity. The scripture reveals that God wants us to know it is He who calls us by name and it is through a revelation of this fact that we have the ability to operate in our highest calling.

In order to operate effectively in your calling, it is essential that you know what is attached to your name. Sometimes it is good to know what the consensus is about you, but it is more important that you know the truth about yourself. Unfortunately, so often we find ourselves doing things that we regret because somewhere along the line we have forgotten, or traded who we were for other things. However, when you come into an awareness of who you were created to be then things will definitely change for the better. In order for this to work you must submit to God and lean on Him.

I want to show you how God went before Esther and made sure things were in order long before she made it to the palace. If you will journey with me, you will see just how big of a God we serve. You will see that He paid attention to every detail from her reality as an orphan, to the time that she would spend in preparation, down to the moment when she would go before the King. In short, God positioned Esther to have favorable circumstances with people to ensure that she would make it to the place of her destiny on time.

The Royal Palace

An extravagant banquet that King Ahasuerus (Xerxes) hosted for all his ministers and officials opens the book of Esther. The scriptures reveal that the King displayed his riches for one hundred and eighty days at the exclusive banquet, and then hosted a smaller, equally extravagant banquet for the people in his immediate community of Susa. Esther 1:6-7 describes the scenery so beautifully:

> *There were curtains (draperies) of fine white and violet linen fastened with cords of fine purple linen to silver rings and marble columns. The couches of gold and silver rested on a mosaic floor of porphyry, marble, mother-of-pearl, and precious colored stones. Drinks were served in various kinds of golden goblets, and the royal wine was plentiful, in accordance with the generosity of the king.*

Who wouldn't want to be a part of such a grandiose event? I'm sure the fellowship was amazing, but the beauty of the palace's decorations is breathtaking. The colors of the fabrics, the high marble pillars, and the mosaic pavement are so welcoming that it might cause one to act like royalty even if only for one day. Aesthetically, this is definitely a banquet fit for people of royalty, whether or not indicated by their socio-economic class.

But, how do we move an orphan girl like Esther to this arena permanently? How can her lifestyle be merged with one that is higher than possibly anything she ever dreamed? I'm reminded of the scripture in Deuteronomy 6:10-11 where God gives decrees and promises to the children of Israel for their obedience. It says,

> Then it shall come about when the Lord your God brings you into the land which He swore (solemnly promised) to [give] your fathers—to Abraham, Isaac, and Jacob—to give you, [a land with] great and splendid cities which you did not build, and houses full of all good things which you did not fill, and hewn (excavated) cisterns (wells) which you did not dig out, and vineyards and olive trees which you did not plant, and you eat and are full and satisfied, then beware that you do not forget the Lord who brought you out of the land of Egypt, out of the house of slavery.

The word *give* in the Hebrew translates to the word *nâthan*, which means to send forth or send before. Just as Isaiah prophesied in the opening scripture of this chapter that God will go ahead and take care of everything as confirmation to the children of Israel, we see the same promise working long before Esther is introduced. Think back to the description of the palace that would eventually become her home as proof of this promise working.

God intervened on Esther's behalf because of the promises He made collectively to her ancestors and the Jewish people. He positioned her in the palace for the assignment that had her name on it. As I will show in the following chapters, Esther's lineage is very important to her destiny. While the Jews needed a deliverer from their enemies, God wanted to make good on His promise to not only Esther, but the Jewish citizens who refused to bow to other gods. Specifically, though, when God removed the reigning Queen Vashti from her royal place He was delivering on His promise to Esther's family.

Vashti's Removal Prepared Esther's Entrance

In Esther 1, on the seventh day of the second banquet, which was the one for the Susa community, the King, in a drunken state, sent seven eunuchs to summon Queen Vashti. He wanted her to display her beauty before the party's attendees. Perhaps the only reason the King summoned her was to feed his ego further. He may have thought, "why not add the prized woman to the long list of things that I can do?" Whatever the King's reasons were, Vashti interrupted them when she refused his summoning. The Bible tells us that she was hosting her own party and probably wanted to continue her time with guests. However, this is the first time we see anyone disobey the King, and it is odd that Vashti refused him because he ruled in a totalitarian fashion. To put this in context, she said no to a man who could literally kill her on the spot and she knew it! I am sure she was aware that this would anger him and that there was a possibility that she would be punished, but that didn't matter. The facts warrant the question as to why she would take a risk with her life. The only logical reason is God!

When God needs a work done in the earth, He will move people around in order to see it fulfilled. The Lord knew the things that would transpire in the future and needed Esther in place to ensure that His will was carried out. Ultimately, there is no other reason as to why Vashti would react uncharacteristically to a simple request. Therefore, it is important to remember that God does not only cause good things to happen, but He also causes hard things to happen. I know this may be a difficult reality to wrap your head around, but it's not farfetched because Jesus openly says in Matthew 10:34 that He did not come to the earth to bring peace but a sword. Hence, when important transitions need to happen, God will cause people to act strangely in order to get a desired end result.

Just as He did with Vashti—caused her to say no—He will do with you! When God wants you to change, He will cause you to act in ways you never thought possible. He will literally bring a sword to your inner life and slice, stab, and destroy the things that He doesn't like. He will cause you to be at war inwardly until you submit to His will, and during this time you will experience a level of discomfort that is unexplainable. You may even lose certain fleshly desires because He's cleaning you out. People you once loved to be around may begin to look different, or that relationship that you once found satisfying will change, and all of these things are evidence that God is changing something inside of you. In this type of season, He is calling you higher and demanding a different response, but if you don't respond well there may be consequences.

Unfortunately, Vashti's refusal was met with the result of being stripped of her role as Queen. When the King asked the seven sages, which were his advisors, about the punishment for her they suggested that she be stripped of her queenly status due to her influence over the other women in the province. Ultimately, the sages feared that the other women would follow Vashti's lead and begin to disregard their husbands, so they instructed the King to make a decree that solidified that every man be the authority of his household (Esther 1:16-22). In essence, the sages wanted Vashti to be replaced with someone who was better.

Obedience is a Characteristic of Queens

What makes one better than Vashti, according to the sages' measure? Perhaps the same thing that causes God to favor His children. Obedience. Vashti was disobedient to the King and her disobedience disqualified her reign. In the same way, God requires absolute obedience in every area of our lives. If we are to ever embody who God created us to be then we must submit our will unto Him through obedience. Vashti's punishment from the King serves as a warning parable for us that illustrates a hard truth– if we don't obey the first time there might not be a next time. So, I want to encourage you to purpose in your heart to heed to the promptings of the Holy Spirit immediately because a delayed response is disobedience.

It is interesting that the sages equated a domestic occurrence to a national crisis. Openly, they asked for a gendered law that would sentence other women in the kingdom. Unfortunately, the sages' hearts were impure and they were focused on the laws and legalism, but this was still in the plan of God. He knew that Ahasuerus would consult men who knew the laws of the land and He used their hearts to influence Ahasuerus' actions to ensure Esther's arrival.

Beware of Offense

The King initially had peace about his decision concerning Vashti because he believed that he was making the right choice. However, as time progressed, Esther 2:1 explains that,

> ...after these things, when the wrath of King Ahasuerus had subsided, he remembered Vashti and what she had done and what had been decreed against her.

This means that in his anger of rejection, he made quick decision, but not without remembering Vashti. I want to use the King's actions to illustrate the trap of offense. More than anything, the King was offended by Vashti's refusal because he was embarrassed in front of guests. While he ruled in a totalitarian fashion, when she rejected Him before others, he felt that she had to be made an example of. Nodding to offense, I'm reminded of when Jesus speaks to his disciples in Luke 17. Jesus tells them that they should consistently forgive those who offend them— even if they do so seven times a day. The disciples then respond asking the Lord to increase their faith. I used to, and still sometimes do, feel like the disciples. By this time, they witnessed miracles, signs, and wonders but hadn't uttered that they needed their faith increased. Yet, when Jesus commands absolute and repetitive forgiveness, they need their faith increased— and quick! The disciples do not try to clarify Jesus' command, seek deeper understanding on how it might work, or even ask Him to repeat it, but immediately ask for more faith. That story is comforting because it shows me that I'm not alone in my daily struggle to shake off offense, but it also challenges me to overcome human proclivities that may stagnate me. In the same way, you should feel encouraged too because the same grace extends to you.

Though the disciples' response is understandable, I want to bring it back to the main point of the offense. Vashti offended the King and he responded in anger. If offense is unchecked it can hinder one from fulfilling their true purpose. It can also deter you from acting in obedience to the command of God. With this in mind, in *The Bait of Satan: Living Free from the Deadly Trap of Offense,* John Bevere asserts that many people have difficulty functioning properly in their purpose because of the wounds that offense has caused. He explains that,

> *Often their conclusions are drawn from inaccurate information. Or their information is accurate, but their conclusion is distorted.*

The King suffers from the latter, which is a distorted conclusion. While he believes that his decree is only for the gain of the men in the kingdom, he fails to realize that God used him to bring His plan to earth. Ultimately, God orchestrated the entire thing and positioned the major players for His plan to be executed. Interestingly, on the seventh day of the second banquet, the King sent seven eunuchs to Vashti, and on the same seventh day he inquired of the seven sages for the best way to handle their conflict. In the Bible, seven is the number of completion, which demonstrates that the stage has been completely set for Esther to enter after these events transpired. It also signals that she was cleared to enter into the first phase of her destiny process.

Wisdom that Leads to Repentance

As I look back over my life, I can see the truth of how God arranges our future arenas. Every time I got my little feelings hurt because someone rejected me it was God preparing the way. Every time that I was on punishment I was forced to find something to do at home and this was God going before me. In the same way that God was using the rejection to show me the value of relationship with Him, my mother was using punishment to teach me a lesson for misbehaving as God was honing my gift and love for writing. Because I've always been drawn to narratives and I find joy in writing, I majored in English literature. What I didn't know is that the long term papers, exams, and scholarly articles would prepare me for this moment... the moment where I would humble myself long enough to sit at the feet of the Father to learn why I like to read, write, and teach certain subjects.

I wish that I could say that I came into the fullness of my identity when I got saved, but I didn't. In fact, I was hell-bent on not fulfilling the call on my life and was very rebellious. Thankfully, God didn't give up on me and neither will He give up on you. Because He's a loving God who is patient with us even when we outright defy His commands, He welcomes us back when we walk away from Him and He comforts us even in the midst of our punishment. I'm so thankful that He keeps His initial plans for us no matter how long it takes us to realize them and that He has greatness in store for everyone, including you, yes you! I want you to know that there is nothing that you can do to pluck yourself out of God's hands, but you *can decide* to walk away from Him. In fact, you can choose to *forgo your destiny* and witness someone else live out theirs, but I don't think that would be beneficial for you. So I encourage you to submit to God so that He may do a good work through you, reveal your identity, and reveal your destiny.

Perhaps, you have noticed a tug in your spirit calling you out of your mess. It may seem like an itch you can't scratch or discontentment while you're trying to be satisfied, or maybe it's unrest when you're supposed to have peace. If you experience these things it means that God is calling you to come higher in Him! He is leading you to the stage set just for you...

but you must be willing to go.

In addition to obedience, one essential key in realizing your royal place is repenting of your sins and turning away from them. It is true that sin can blind you to so many things, including bad relationships. So many times, women have the tendency to fall into the entitlement trap in regards to relationships that prevent us from moving. I know this because I was once one of them, but I want to encourage you to leave that toxic relationship or anything else alone, and commit to a life of purity and watch God give you beauty for ashes.

If you will, I want to tell you a quick story on how I began to realize my royal arena. While this is not the exhaustive story, the highlights will hopefully assist you in understanding how I recognized it. In order to do so, I intertwine my spiritual journey with my physical journeys and educational pursuits, because they inform one another. In retrospect, it seemed that at any given moment it could be the best of times and the worst of times at the same time. While I was excelling in one area of my life I would be failing miserably in another and constantly negotiating between two spheres. Hopefully my story will help you understand the tensions and stutters in my life and how I overcame them, which will in turn allow you to take personal inventory.

Realizing My Arena

I've always been viewed as an anomaly, and in the past I considered it a curse because I hated standing out like a sore thumb. I used to question God about why He made me this way and wondered why He allowed people to see my difference. As a result of the pain of not fitting in, I began to take on the ways of others as I attempted to run from who God created me to be. If you can imagine a chameleon that changes colors to blend with its environment, then you've envisioned me. But, the danger that I wanted to hide from was the essence of who I was and it caused me great pain to cast off.

Looking back over my life, I didn't want to be a leader. I didn't want to be positive. I surely didn't want to be seen as a Jesus freak. I wanted to be the cool girl, the bad chick, and the Instagram model that was desired but never touched. I wanted to be smart AND dumb, in an attempt to become a walking contradiction, and all these things I became. However, when I finally reached the point that I was striving towards, the green grass wasn't as pleasing as I thought. Granted, I had the grades and was perceived as smart, but the inner trouble that comes with trying to be like others left me with many restless nights. I wanted to "sleep it away, drink it away, and sex it away," but nothing worked! Eventually, I didn't recognize the woman in the mirror. I didn't think it was I who needed to change, but the world. The distorted image of the dying woman looking back at me was someone I didn't really recognize as my inner self. She, in the mirror, was ugly, beaten, rejected, and thought everyone better than her. I, on the other hand, was an A student in the relationship of my dreams, and made it out of Chicago. I had major accomplishments, bragging rights, and I was fly, or so I thought. I became the contradiction that I tried so hard to embody, but the aftermath left me defeated and in tears. I traded myself for the approval of others and I left my identity on the side of the road challenging it to find its way back to me. Needless to say, my identity didn't come find me, *but I had to go in search of it.*

In retrospect, I believe God allowed me to achieve everything that I wanted just to realize that it was unfulfilling. I couldn't use another man to fix my daddy issues. I couldn't pile the foundation thick enough on my face to hide my insecurities. I definitely couldn't find my destiny in the turn up. Shockingly, I couldn't get another degree to silence my feeling of inadequacy and abandonment, and there was no external thing that could anesthetize my trauma. What I DID discover in pursuing those things outside of God was more pain.

I experienced a lot of agony because I knew that what I was doing was wrong! I struggled between wanting to be "normal" and being different, even though I never qualified what normalcy actually meant. Normalcy, in many respects, is a state of mind and not a measurement of destiny. Unfortunately, what people don't tell you is that you will pay with your thirties and forties for the actions, or lack thereof, in your twenties.

What Running Has the Potential to Do to You

I didn't really enjoy a life contrary to who God destined to me to be and I'm glad He didn't allow me to. While I knew one day it might come to a point of total surrender, I wasn't sure how I could move from this to that. I didn't know how I could manage to embrace my calling when I struggled against it for so long. I was also terrified to admit that I had come to the end of myself, so I kept pushing myself harder.

My fear and outright disregard for the promptings of God led me straight to anxiety. Anxiety is likened to the ability to pre-worry, and because I was in school, working several jobs and still running from God, I pushed myself to perform even when my body was shutting down. I don't think it was the stress of school that was unbearable, but it was the weight of God closing in on me. This time He was not giving up and I knew it. I knew He was tired of playing with me. Tired of waiting and seeing me live like an orphan when I was birthed into His family. He was calling me with great clarity to an arena that I only saw in quick visions but I didn't want that life completely. I couldn't run anymore and I didn't have anywhere to go either. God literally pulled a sword on me and had me cornered. In that moment, I had to choose to either submit to His will or submit to the medication doctors prescribed me for anxiety and depression. I was conflicted because I felt that I shouldn't need medication. I felt that I shouldn't need a pill to help me sleep and manage my emotions, but also didn't want to feel the anxiety long before the situation arose. I thought that I was going crazy! I questioned and wondered if I took the pills if I would I need them for the rest of my life.

Listen, I want you to understand that mental health is serious. Sometimes women push the weight of their reality off to save others, but I want to encourage you that if you need to see a healthcare provider, do so. If you feel that you need counseling, you should get it and not wait until you come to the end of your rope and are left to figure things out alone. Luckily, I had some phenomenal people around to help me see my situation clearly. While they didn't give me the revelation of what I'm sharing with you, they did talk to me about self-neglect, which is a serious offense to yourself.

However, they weren't the only ones talking in this season; God also had a lot to say. He asked me if I would keep running from His call and then demanded that I listen to the hard truth that I was becoming bitter and hardhearted. He revealed that I started to take on a pessimistic attitude and had been running on fumes for majority of my life. He asked, "Briana, who would you become if you trusted Me? How much success would you have if you included Me in your decisions?" I want you to take a moment to ask yourself the same questions God asked me. I want you to seriously reflect on them because they can potentially begin the process that He has been speaking to you about.

In my case, God revealed that I was battling depression and anxiety because I was walking in blatant disobedience. Now, I am not saying that this is the case for everyone, but I am saying that this was true for me. My choices led me to a point of desperation and shame and I didn't want to be like that anymore. I didn't want to paint the smile on my face and inwardly cry. I didn't want to tell people that I was great when I wasn't. I wanted to be better. I wanted to be more. I wanted to be honest. I wanted to become who God created me to be, and hopefully you have similar desires.

Like Esther, my Royal arena was set and God positioned me according to His will. It took years to get me to this point, but I had to get to a place of desperation, irritation, and complete discomfort in order to be prepared for this moment. The setting of your arena might look distinctively different from Esther's and mine and that's ok! I'm sure if you pay close enough attention to your past you can see the hand of God orchestrating things for you. I want you to understand that only YOU can reject your royal arena– as you have the power to walk in and out of it anytime you want– but that might not be the best thing to do. Therefore, you must partner with God in this process and it starts with a heart of obedience.

Welcome to your royal courts!

Chapter Two

IDENTITY

Then God said, 'Let Us (Father, Son, Holy Spirit) make man in Our image, according to Our likeness [not physical, but a spiritual personality and moral likeness]'...So God created man in His own image, in the image and likeness of God He created him; male and female He created them.

Genesis 1:26-7

Has someone ever told you that you resemble your mom or dad? Perhaps they told you that you act like one or the other when you do certain things. You may even be referred to as acting like someone who died before you were born. Generally, people's perceptions of our parents or ancestors determine how they see us, and if their understanding is skewed, then it may impact certain outcomes in our lives. This idea is definitely true in spiritual battles.

Genesis 1:26-27 tells us that we are made in the image of the Father, Son, and Holy Spirit. This means that we have similar mannerisms, thought processes, and moral proclivities to our

Father in heaven. But, sometimes when our perception of our identity is flawed, it is difficult to see the whole picture, and we struggle horribly to healthily discern if the parts that we inherited from our parents are in direct opposition to Him. It is hard to decipher if our familial characteristics are causing us to live beneath who we were created to be because they are the very traits that are used to identify us as kin. The battle then becomes one of deciding whether to cater to our identity in God or our parents. There was a time that I had difficulty deciding between the two, which is why I chose the familial lifestyle that I was most familiar with. It is quite intriguing that the words *family* and *familiar* are spelled almost exactly alike. The Latin spelling of the word family, *familia*, connotes to be a servant of a household, while familiar means to be close and intimate; however, further research of familiar leads back to family.

I think it is telling that these words are almost synonymous with one another, especially since our familial ties sometimes hold us hostage. Sometimes, the familiar is dangerous and counterproductive to our progress as we attempt to follow Christ. I would also go as far as to suggest that familiar familial ties have the power to stagnate our lives in ways that other relationships cannot. Therefore, we have to recognize that in order to be successful in our pursuit of God, we have to figure out which characteristics He entrusted us with, and which are the hindrances from ancestral lineages. I must admit that this will not be an easy thing to do because the normalcy of our family seduces us to come back to the comfort of its hold, but we have to do something different if we hope to live differently. Sometimes what we don't realize is that God, the devil, and our families are always competing for our understanding of identity. These three opposing voices will each show you the benefits of following their path, but each benefit will not be in your best interest.

With this in mind, this chapter is designed to walk you through an in-depth understanding of your identity. It looks at the ways in which our familial lineage opens us up to blessings and curses, and it highlights the ways in which our awareness of personal ancestral lineages has the ability to taint or positively impact our perception of why we were created. Ultimately, I want you to understand that though your arena is set, there are factors that have the potential to either set you up for success or failure. Pay close attention to the information presented and try to relate it to your life in a constructive manner. At times it may seem that I'm giving you a lot of information, but it's to help you understand how many layers God has to remove in order for you to fully embody the person He had in mind. While some of the layers are not your fault, they are your responsibility.

Descended from the Benjamities

"Now in Shushan the palace there was a certain Jew, whose name was Mordecai, the son of Jair, the son of Shimei, the son of Kish, a Benjamite."

Esther 2:5

Before Esther is introduced, her cousin Mordecai and lineage through which he was birthed is referenced as illustrated in Esther 2:5. At the time, Mordecai was a royal official serving in the King's court, which means that he has a pretty high ranking in the citadel. Perhaps, what is more interesting is that he is a

Benjamite. For context, the Benjamites are one of the twelve tribes of Israel in the Old Testament, and were named after Benjamin who is the younger son of Jacob and Rachel (Genesis 35:24). Benjamin's father Jacob is the one who leveraged his brother Esau's birthright from Him in a weak moment (Genesis 25), and the same Jacob who was tricked by his uncle Laban into marrying Leah, the woman he did not labor seven years for (Genesis 29:23). Upon realizing that he was tricked, he labored seven more years for his prized bride Rachel who was barren until the Lord opened her womb and gave her Joseph, and eventually Benjamin (Genesis 30:22). Unfortunately, moments after childbirth, while on the way to Jerusalem Rachel dies, and before she takes her last breath she names the baby Benoni, which means "my pain," a name that alludes to the state of Rachel right before she died. Jacob overruled the cursed name and renamed his son Benjamin that means "son of the right hand." The right hand speaks to power and grace that are all characteristics of Benjamin.

Historical Overview of the Benjamites

The Benjamites were men of valor in the Old Testament and mighty men of war. When Jacob blesses his sons before death in Genesis 49:27 he says,

> *Benjamin is a ravenous wolf; in the morning he devours the prey, and at night he divides the spoil.*

If you study the Benjamites, you'll discover that they had capabilities to destroy their enemies. They were skilled archers and left-handed warriors, and their bravery coupled with the ability to attack their enemies unaware deemed them a serious threat.

The fact that Mordecai was a descendant of the tribe foreshadows his ability to expose the enemy unaware. The enemy of the Jews is later identified as Haman and the enemies of the King were his eunuchs who guarded the door—Bigthan and Teresh—that conspired to attack him. Neither the eunuchs nor Haman knew that Mordecai was the person who exposed their evil plans, but when he learned of the eunuchs' plans against the King, he told Queen Esther and they were punished. Mordecai was eventually rewarded for his discovery and recognized as the man who saved the King's life. In regard to Haman and his plan, he had no idea that he was in trouble and thought he was being honored when he was exposed.

Nevertheless, I want to point out the lineage of Mordecai because it is essential to the identity of Esther. The scripture reveals that Esther's father was Mordecai's uncle and this means he was also associated with the tribe of Benjamin. And, if her father was associated with Benjamin then she too has the Benjamite blood coursing through her veins.

Esther's Direct Ancestral Links

> *"Now as for Esther, the daughter of Abihail the uncle of Mordecai who had taken her in as his [own] daughter..."*
> Esther 2:15

Though Esther is introduced a little earlier in the scripture (Esther 2:9) when the virgins were called to the King, the Bible backs up a bit to reveal the identity of her father. Esther was the daughter of Mordecai's uncle Abihail.

In the Hebrew, Esther's father's name, Abihail, means "my father is might." His name originates from the prefix *ab* and suffix *chayil*. *Chayil* in the Hebrew is associated with wealth, force, virtue, and influence. Yet, in its feminine sense it is connected to ability. As you keep reading you will notice that Esther had the ability to do things that other women could not do in those days. As she submitted her spirit and actions to the will of God she was graced with several abilities. Through her life we have the opportunity to bear witness to the power of an obedient spirit.

Esther's father's name and its meaning are necessary to understand that Esther comes from a strong lineage whether she realizes it or not. Lineages are very important to us because they can provide clues to the outcomes of our lives. Think about it: at a doctor's appointment they ask that patients fill out a questionnaire about the history of their family. At minimum the doctor seeks information about three generations of people in one's family. This is not simply happenstance, but highlights an understanding of the importance of familial ties. Ultimately, doctors understand that families have a lot in common including genes, environment, and livelihoods. Taken together, these may provide clues to generational ailments that may surface in a family. By investigating these patterns healthcare professionals can determine if an individual, other family members, or future members are susceptible to developing certain conditions.

If this is true in the natural it is definitely true spiritually. If you can, think about people in your family who have distinctive commonalities. Perhaps all the men in your family die prematurely or all the women in your family seem to get pregnant out of wedlock. Any and all of the commonalities may be clues about what has attached itself to your family lineage and what is after you. Personally, I descend from a line of strong black women who are single mothers. When I say strong, I mean strong in every sense of the word. Again, this is a common trait, but just because it is normal in my family doesn't mean it is right. In essence, anything outside of the will of God or His initial plan for a thing is perverted. I want to challenge you to spend time locating the lineage commonality in your family and test that characteristic against the Bible to see if it aligns. Basically you will ask God to reveal any hindrances to your life that are a result of your familial lineage. You should record anything he shows you or anything that comes to mind. And, those things that don't come into alignment with the Word of God is wrong no matter how normal it may seem.

With this in mind, Proverbs 14:12 reminds us that there is a way that seems right to us but its end is death. Unbeknownst to many, there are things in our lives or the lives of others that may die due to actions, beliefs, or mindsets. In essence, the phrase "that's just the way that I am" or "this is how it's always been" is devastatingly inaccurate. Please hear me, people have not always been the way that they are now. Instead, something happened to cause them to take on the ways of others. To make this plain, we generally learn the behavior or adopt the ideology to which we presently ascribe in response to something else. I want to challenge you to seek God and ask Him to reveal to you the person He created in your mother's womb, and ask Him to restore to you the image of who you were called to be. The truth is that sometimes we take on the ways of others for so long that it becomes part of our personality, but those things that you've picked up along the way are not who you are, *but what you've allowed to become a part of you.*

My Familial Realization

A couple of years ago, I noticed the same characteristics of strength surface in my life. While I believe that strength in the proper context is necessary, when it functions to overrule your relationship with God it is wrong. When God revealed the reality of the error of my ways and my flawed perception of strength, I rejected the knowledge. I have to admit that it wasn't just strength that God was revealing, but also toxic attitudes. I honestly believe that the spirit of strength that traveled through my family lineage was used to operate in spite of God. He promised us to never leave nor forsake us (Deuteronomy 31:6), but in the strength of our bodies, we became the gods of our lives.

I am so grateful that God revealed this trait to me long ago, and since then I've made the conscious effort to keep my life in alignment with His word. A little while ago, I committed to memory 2 Corinthians 12:10:

> *So I am well pleased with weaknesses, with insults, with distresses, with persecutions, and with difficulties, for the sake of Christ; for when I am weak [in human strength], then I am strong [truly able, truly powerful, truly drawing from God's strength].*

The scripture reveals that there is a difference between human strength and God's strength. In essence, human strength is weakness compared to the strength that God gives us, but when I first attempted to understand the significance of the scripture, I struggled because I couldn't figure out how it worked. I, of course, operated in my own strength for a long time but I wanted the strength that the scripture talks about. I wanted to draw strength from the power source, but it required me to abandon my will for His. Ultimately, I had to position myself, with the help of the Holy Spirit, to submit my life to God and come into complete obedience with His plan for me.

For me, it meant no dating for a year. While it might seem a bit drastic it was necessary. I literally cut off all the men who were pursuing me, the guys who were just filling up empty space in my life, and the ones who were just randoms for when I got bored. I had to block their numbers, social media accounts, and even emails because I knew that bad choices in men ran through my family. It was a hard thing for me to do back then, but the freedom that I experienced as a result is worth so much more. People told me that I was crazy to do something so uncommon but desperate times call for desperate measures. Your thing might not be men, it may be food, lesbianism, or lying, but whatever it is, you must surrender it unto the Lord.

Just as certain traits follow families for several generations, the Lord gives a promise in Psalm 105:8 that He remembers His covenant and promises for a thousand generations. Today we measure a generation by twenty-five years or so, and if this understanding is applied to the scripture, it means that God's word will be fulfilled from 25,000 years prior. I wonder how far back we would have to travel to see the original promise in our families. Would we even know to whom the promise was made? Thinking about the children of Israel, God made several promises to them and we are privy to the ramifications of some of them as revealed in Esther's father's name: wealth, virtue, influence, and force. These same characteristics are the inheritance of Esther through direct familial lineage association; therefore, she was destined for such a time as this.

Perception of Identity

Psychoanalysts agree that parents are essential in helping to develop the identity of a child. While it is a blessing that Mordecai raised Esther, let's look deeper at the effects of her parents' death. Esther is left to figure out her identity alone because her mother serves as her connection and bond to the world. In most cases, mothers represent the nurturing side of our maturation as they are the comforters and secret keepers. At a young age, they present a mirror image for who we may become. On the other hand, a father in a young woman's life serves several purposes. The father is the first man that she will love and he sets the standard for how all men should treat her as she grows up. His presence in her life is crucial, to say the least, especially in the developmental and teenage years.

I can attest to the importance of having both parents in my life. My mother, in many ways, groomed me to be the woman I am today, while my father was not around as much as I would have liked. In his absence, I was left to figure out how a man's touch should or should not feel. I struggled with having healthy relationships because coming from a single parent home I saw my mom do everything, and I assumed that I would have to do the same for a man to love me. More times than not, my identity became intertwined in dead-end relationships and I thought that I was looking for a man to love me, but in reality

I was looking for the love of my father. When those relationships failed I felt the void of my dad over and over again. The absence of my father further led me to subconsciously feel that people abandoned me because of who I was.

I must be clear in that my father never abandoned me, but in my childish reasoning I perceived that he did. In my limited perspective, I dated and attempted to fix my father through men. I would attempt to manipulate the men into staying with me by being overly emotional. I would beg them to love me and give myself over freely just to feel something. I really wanted those men then, but more than ever I wanted my dad. Unfortunately, I did not know how to communicate that to him effectively so I willingly embarked on a path of self-destruction. My willingness was unconscious because on the surface I clung to the belief that I was committed to healthy relationships. The truth is that I was committed to dysfunction that had become my normal.

If you can recognize any truth in my explanation, I urge you to take some time to comb through your past experiences and attempt to locate where these trends ring true for you. I want you to consider how you may have contributed to past hurts, and/or allowed your childhood to dictate your adult responses. Think about the times when you may have lashed out at someone, but were subconsciously talking to someone else. It is important that we get healed from these wounds if we ever hope to fully become a Woman of Royalty.

Just like Esther, though I came from a mighty lineage, I couldn't recognize the importance of who I was due to past circumstances. The magnitude of an absent parent seemed to haunt me in everything that I endeavored to do. By the same token, I believe one reason that Esther struggled with her identity is because she was an orphan and struggled with self-esteem, love, and peace. In fact, the Bible presents Esther's condition perfectly:

> [Mordecai] was the guardian of Hadassah, that is Esther, his uncle's daughter, for she had no father or mother. The young woman was beautiful of form and face; and when her father and mother died, Mordecai took her in as his own daughter (Esther 2:7).

Esther's external condition of having neither father nor mother sandwiches the essence of who she is in Christ. Let's look back at the scripture for a moment because I want to walk you through the way it was revealed to me.

We can interpret Esther 2:7 in multiple ways: One way is that *others* thought Esther was beautiful in form and face, which would highlight the severity of her inability to push past the death of her parents. Perhaps, her loneliness overshadowed her identity and while others can see the beauty of who she is, she cannot. There are moments where our vision may be skewed because of the high trees in the forest. We may struggle to really perceive who we are due to life's circumstances even though people tell us how wonderful we are. Unfortunately, their encouragement does not amount to the magnitude of our experiences and we reject their comfort. Perhaps, you're aware of how you really are, and therefore, you struggle to accept the way others see you. I know I can relate to those feelings. Though I wasn't an orphan as Esther, I did feel abandoned and neglected, which impacted my life negatively.

Another way that the Holy Spirit revealed the scripture to me was in the way that Esther sees herself versus the way God sees her. Because we are fearfully and wonderfully made, God sees the beauty of who we are even when we are acting less than beautiful. Jeremiah 1:5 magnifies the reality of how God sees us:

> *Before I formed you in the womb I knew you [and approved of you as My chosen instrument], And before you were born I consecrated you [to Myself as My own]; I have appointed you as a prophet to the nations.*

This scripture really resonates with me because it shows that we are chosen. God chose us before our parents got together, before we were teased in school, and even when we decided to disobey Him. Not only are we chosen, but we are approved, consecrated and appointed! Jeremiah tells us that we don't have to seek the approval of others because God has already given His. We do not have to try to be someone else because God has already consecrated us, nor do we have to seek a position because ours was already created before we were born. Ultimately, this is great news because it puts to rest the taunting thoughts of inadequacy that so many people struggle to overcome. The person who God created before we were born is who He communicates with. He does not lower Himself to our insecurities, nor does He participate in our pity parties. Instead He calls us higher and holds us to the standard of who He created us to be, and continues to speak to the person He had in mind when He formed us. Thankfully, He is not overly concerned with what happened to us in the past, but is more interested in what He can do through us. And, though He is sympathetic to our infirmities, He is not bound by the reality of our situations.

Like Esther, I struggled horribly with identity. Though other people would affirm me, I still felt low. I felt that no one really understood what I was going through. It also seemed as if I were wondering helplessly through life with no chance of change. In retrospect, I was wrong and was reasoning through the lens of pain, but it wasn't until God brought me to the threshing floor that I realized the errors of my ways.

I wish I could give you a time frame of when things will shift, but that would be dishonest of me and I think you deserve better than that. I do want to let you know that there is an expiration date for your present circumstance. While I know things began to change in 2013 when I was baptized, the process is still ongoing. There are still things that God shows me about my identity that I am in awe of, and He consistently highlights the toxins that I have picked up along the way, which challenges me to do the work of becoming better.

Ultimately, we have to find our identity in God and not our jobs, who we care for, new shoes, and other things that will pass away. What a tragedy it would be if you died not knowing who you really were. What if you live a life that is completely beneath you but don't know it? Perhaps you do know it, but don't know the first place to start. A good place to begin is to acknowledge that we must trust that God knows who we are created to be. I guarantee that if you surrender to His promptings you will discover the mystery of who you are, but it starts with obedience.

Obedience will lead you to your identity. The word *identity* does not appear in the Bible, but *image* does. In the Hebrew, *image* means reflecting some of God's own perfections: perfect in knowledge, righteousness and holiness; therefore, we are made in the perfect image of God reflecting His righteousness and holiness. While all of our choices may not mirror Christ, we were initially created blameless and holy. With this in mind, Psalm 39:6 that talks about how men walk around like a shadow when they are seeking things of the world. In correlation, the word *tselem* means to be as a shadow of a thing, which represents the original very imprecisely. Or it means merely a phantom, which means to represent the original more closely but lacks its essential characteristic or reality. Unfortunately, our sin nature makes us look like a phantom in the shadow of God, and though we were created in His image, our image became distorted with the fall of man. Though seemingly unrecognizable, God calls out to the deep in us, which is the part that He still identifies with. Yet, He used His son to bridge the gap between He and us. Now, I don't know about you but I sure am glad that He did it! We shouldn't want to walk around looking like a bootleg copy of a great original. Instead, we should desire to be restored to mirror the beauty and the timelessness of the creator. If this is your heart's desire, then I want you to get before the Lord and seek His plan for your life.

Chapter Three

YOUR NAME CARRIES FAVOR

"For I know the plans and thoughts that I have for you, says the Lord, 'plans for peace and well-being and not for disaster to give you a future and a hope."

Jeremiah 29:11

I t is true that your ancestry has the ability to dictate to you the ways in which you live, but when you overcome the generational curses assigned to your last name there is a level of freedom that you will operate in. Once free, you will notice that while you may resemble people in your family, there are some things that only you can do that way that you do it.

Think about this within the context of brand distinction. What makes KFC's chicken different from Popeye's? Yes, they both sell chicken, but the small difference is in their names and their approaches to chicken preparation. KFC advertises that they "Do chicken right" while Popeye's claims to be "Louisiana

Bad." In the same vein, think of McDonalds and Burger King. McDonalds advertises that they "Love to see you smile" while Burger King promises that the establishment will let you "Have it your way." Though each competitor may sell similar products, their names classify them as operating in a class by themselves. You cannot go to KFC and ask for Popeyes' seasoned fries, nor can you go to McDonalds demanding a whopper with cheese because their names tell you what they carry, and if you want what the competitor has then you must go where you see their name.

   The same is true for your name and what is attached to it. Many of us don't realize that there are things attached to our name, or if we do it is only in the context of a reputation. While I agree that reputations are important, they are not the only things attached to you. I remind you that Esther had a name before she found her purpose. Before she realized her name was Hadassah (Jewish name) she had an attachment to it. We learn of her name long before we learn of Esther's ability to save the Jews. This is strategic because it is impossible to know our charge in the world without first discovering who we are and why we were created. We cannot help people if we don't understand what we carry and why it's so precious. God wants to give us a future and a hope but we might not recognize it due to our inability to see ourselves clearly. In Esther's case, before she speaks in the scriptures, she is introduced and her background is told. Think of this in relation to a speaker at a conference. Generally, there is someone to introduce the speaker before they come to the microphone, right? Well the same is true for us. God goes before us to speak and introduce us to the world long before we reach a platform, write a book, or anything else. However, the way that God introduces us is in correlation to how we were created, not how we see ourselves. So I ask you, "Do you know your name?"

Significance of a Name

Esther's Jewish name is Hadassah and it translates into the word myrtle. A Myrtle plant produces a fragrant essential oil as it grows in the northern Mediterranean region and the Sahara Desert. The oil of the plant carries the essence of the plant's fragrance and an understanding of this will help to understand the importance of identity. In Esther's case, the name Hadassah carries the oil needed to procure the safety of the Jews in the next couple chapters. This is another clue that the scene was already set for her long before she reached the kingdom. God knew that Esther would be the one to set the Jews free, so He imbued her with the capacity and ability to do so.

She was destined to become Queen and defeat those who came against the people of God. She had a divine appointment with destiny and you do too! While she had to experience the same process as the other virgins, she did not have to fight for the crown, which nods back to the love of God for us. In fact, I would go as far to say that the crown already had her name on it, and that Queen Vashti was only borrowing because Esther's position was created before she was born and solidified with the name that her parents gave. I frequently hear people say, "God has a blessing with your name on it?" But, rarely if ever, had I wondered when my name was placed on the blessing. Was this a new blessing or did I fall into a trap where God had to hurry up and design a blessing for me? I now believe that God already had the blessing with my name on it long before I was born. Remember, He knew us before the foundations of the world; therefore, when the blessing comes, it is assigned to the name we were given. Literally, the blessing will be in the spot at the right time and the right place seeking the person whose name is attached to it, but you have to be in position to receive it! More importantly, you have to have the ability to recognize your name (i.e. your identity). If only you'll trust God and through obedience come into alignment with Him you will experience His glory. You are the answer to someone's prayer. You are the change that you seek to see in the world. Your name carries enough weight!

The Essence and Work Attached to a Name

It is interesting that in order for the leaves on the Myrtle plant to be cultivated into the beautiful petals colored in white with berries and seeds that are blue, black and yellow, the plant needs to be exposed to a long hot summer. The plant needs not only to be planted in a certain region, but the region needs to be hot enough to help it produce its flowers. In the same vein, there are moments in everyone's life where we run from the environment needed to produce the greatest fruits. We don't necessarily want to bear the weight of changing, nor do we relish the idea of being uncomfortable. Yet, the cultivating environment for the plant is crucial and so is your environment. I know that when God has you in the fire it can seem unbearable, but the temperature of the fire signals the weight of the glory. I want to encourage you not to attempt to circumvent the process, but endure the time because it will make a positive difference in your life.

I'm reminded of the parable that Jesus speaks John 15:1-2:

I am the true Vine, and My Father is the vinedresser. Every branch in Me that does not bear fruit, He takes away; and every branch that continues to bear fruit, He [repeatedly] prunes, so that it will bear more fruit [even richer and finer fruit].

He's saying that if the plant does not bear fruit, then His Father uproots it and takes it away. However, even if it does bear fruit it must be purged in order to bear more fruit. Now I understand why the plant that does not bear fruit needs to be banished, but why does the one that is bearing need to be purged? I would think that if it were producing then it should be left alone in order to continue producing, right? Well, the Holy Spirit reminded me of the scripture in Isaiah 55:8 that lets us know that God's thoughts and ways are not equivalent to our own. When we are in the situation, we might not see the bigger picture and it is only in hindsight that we understand the past. There have been numerous times that I couldn't see past the trees in the forest. There were moments that I literally thought that I would die due to the weight of the situation and God didn't spare me the pain. Instead, He used it, the disappointment, and the agony to strengthen me and teach me a lesson in obedience. While I wish that I could say that I learned my lesson the first time, I did not, but each time that I got burned by the fire I learned not to play with it.

Going back to Luke 15, the word for purge in the Greek is *kathairo*, which means to cleanse from filth of impurity. Though the plant produces, there are times where it must be purged due to the elements around it. Daily, plants come into contact with harsh elements and it must be cleaned. In the same way, humans also come into contact frequently with impurities such as the music we listen to, the relationships into which we enter, the broken families, hurt, pain, and disappointments, and they all leave their marks, no matter how small, on our spirits. Whether we realize it or not, we carry these things with us, and sometimes, if we are not careful we spread the disease. Though we may be successful in lots of areas, we can still be impure in our spirits. We can even have everything going for us and still be poor in our spirits. We can still have a vindictive and controlling attitude though we look like a million dollars. And there are so many dangerous outcomes of the façade that people portray that are not only hazardous to them, but those who innocently come into their lives.

The Difference Between the Myrtle and the Weed

Sometimes I wonder why the women on certain reality television shows have so much drama, though they appear to live elaborate lifestyles. I contemplate about possible reasons as to why they sit around and gossip. Though they may not have been friends before the show, there is a type of identity that they form collectively. Lots of them convene on hurt deep in their spirit that explodes when the cameras are on. The gossip that they participate in is only lighter fluid to the already simmering fire. Unfortunately, the women cast their lots before the world in an attempt to obtain natural wealth. They trade the true essence of themselves for temporary gains and their actions are weedy. Please hear me, God does not want us to aspire to live like that. Yes, He wants us to live wealthy and fulfilled lives because we are His children, but He does not want us to operate from a level of dysfunction. He wants us to be recognizable to Him and not a phantom version of who we could have been. He wants to make us pure again, free of toxic waste that we have harbored over the years.

God wants us to be like the Myrtle plant but cleansing is inevitable. The plant's purging in the Saharan Desert summer with blazing weather of nearly 120 degrees Fahrenheit is extreme. Though hot, humid, and wildly uncomfortable it is the environment needed for the plant to produce. Naturally, humans may complain of the blaring heat index of the desert because that is not the environment we were designed to be in for lengthy periods of time. The plant, however, never complains. Though it cannot speak, look at its actions as it produces and does so beautifully!

My Name's Cleansing Process

There were times when God had me in the fire that I thought threatened my life. There were times when I went to sleep and awoke feeling exhausted. There was also a lengthy period of time that I didn't recognize myself because I was becoming more like Christ. While I believe that the people who were around me love me and only want the best for me, some of their remarks didn't align with my journey. In fact, there were moments where people told me that I needed to allow myself to live and enjoy my 20's. On the outside looking in, perhaps I was a bit extreme to them, but that's only because God set a standard for my life that they didn't know. I couldn't do the things that they encouraged because I had clear direction from God on how to endure the season. Sometimes I sit and reflect on what would have become of me if I listened to them over the tug in my spirit. Perhaps, this book would not have been written as a result. I want to encourage you not to heed the voice of others over the voice of God.

In relation to the Myrtle plant, what we may see as an inconvenience the plant uses as a method for growth. This is why we cannot compare our process to anyone else's process. We cannot look at others' houses through stained glass windows and covet where they are. We cannot use someone else's testimony as a measuring cup to see how long our process will take because their testimony only serves as encouragement, not the formula. We don't know the price of the oil in their alabaster box or the pain that they endured so we should not covet their lives. If I can be honest, there was a time when I wanted to be like other people, which is why I am warning you against it. I yearned for the things they had because it seemed to make them happy, but I didn't know the price they paid to get them. When I found out their price, I wasn't willing to pay to get the gifts just as I'm probably not willing to pay the price that others pay for their spiritual gifts. It is dangerous to play the comparison game because we are not only giving ourselves permission to devalue who we are, but we grant others the permission to devalue us as well. What a tragedy it would be if we went to someone and demanded respect and they refused based on the fact that we've undervalued ourselves first. Let's make the commitment to want better and live better, and a key to that is finding contentment in our own portion by submitting unto the Lord. In essence, our contentment rests in our ability to allow God to cleanse us through our individualized process.

Refining to Gold

In a moment, I'm going to talk about the beautification process that the virgins underwent, but first I want to point out the power and importance of allowing Christ to refine us. Let's think of this in the terms of the process of refining gold. Gold and silver are generally extracted from the same ore. As a result, they are hard to separate due to their chemical similarity. In the past, there were precious metals that contained a mixture of both gold and silver. Due to the great difficulty of separating the two metals, a special method of separation known as gold parting was invented. Through this process silver and other impurities are removed from the gold.

The Miller and Wohlwill methods were the two major processes used for gold parting. Despite which process used, the goal was to rid the gold of the mixtures that may devalue the metal. Though one process would seem to be enough, there are two because one may be better fitting for one type of metal. If you've ever paid attention to gold, you've probably noticed that all bracelets do not look the same. The better the quality of the gold, the higher the price. If we think of the refining process in our lives as the gold refining process we will understand how precious the gifts inside of us are.

For me, the refining process is usually a very rigorous one. There were times when I'd be in the fire for months at a time then would probably have a couple weeks' break before I entered another purging. Admittedly, I cried a lot during these seasons because the fire was burning everything that was unlike God in my life. I was moody a lot of times and I felt like I was schizophrenic. One minute I would be grateful that God saved my life and the next minute I would have a pity party for myself. I didn't understand it then and there are some situations that are still a mystery to me, but I know that I needed the time in the fire.

Because I was tired of the process there were a couple of times when I tried to jump out of the fire. During these times, I would attempt to backslide and turn away from God intentionally, but I didn't rebel successfully. In fact, during my time of rebellion, I heard the voice of the Lord more clearly. I would attempt to go talk to this guy because I was lonely and didn't feel good about myself, or I would try to gossip about this person because I wasn't happy and the Lord would instantly convict me. It was like He was saying, "What are you doing? Why are you intent on becoming a precious metal?"

Like gold parting and the Myrtle plant, heat is required for the best production. The Father applies heat to our lives in order to purify us and in the refining process He cuts the plant to bear more fruit. You will be just like the gold that must be heated in order to separate it from other substances. While the metal mixture was outwardly known as a precious metal, it was still part gold but the mixture of other elements changed its name and substance. Unfortunately, precious metals are not as valuable as the solid forms of gold and silver, and if you choose to stay on the fence about who God created you to be, you might run a similar risk.

Prepare for Separation

During the separation process or the wilderness season, things will fall away from you. Desires that you once had that were toxic will begin to taste bitter. You may still fall, but you won't be able to stay down. You are not where you are going, you are standing in the middle of your past and present. In essence, you are contemplating a destiny moment. I have to be honest and tell you that there will be times when you will crave your dysfunction and you might even entertain it, but I can almost guarantee that it won't be with the same satisfaction.

In this season, the Lord will start revealing and calling you by your destiny name. He does not speak to the person who is weighed down by the cares of the world, but calls you as He did before the beginning of time. When I first heard God call me by my name, I did not recognize it. Granted, I have been called Briana my whole life, but when I trained my ear to hear His calling, it sounded different because He was calling me from a higher place. He was calling my identity forth and I did not want what came with it. He kept calling. Initially, the call was faint and barely noticeable; then it became louder the more time we spent together. I started to recognize my name more and more and I finally recognized myself!

When God starts to refine us, He digs us down to something solid. He keeps digging because if He does not strike a solid place, we will eventually turn back to our wicked ways. He puts us in the dark to develop us kind of like film used to be developed. No light must enter the dark room because it could potentially damage the exposed film before it is developed. In the same way, when God digs us down to our core, He slowly but surely exposes who we are destined to become. Looking back, I despised the digging process because it spanned over roughly three years. During those years, there were moments where I fought the identity attached to my name because I realized that it would cost me a lot to become the woman who

I was destined to be. Granted, I wanted to be great and even wanted to help people, but first God had to help me become pure. In essence, He had to make me like gold.

I want you to be encouraged in knowing that when you go through the fire you are being purged of impurities. Challenge your doubts when you feel that God has forsaken you. Trust the process when you know that you have done everything right and still got the wrong results. It is only through the process that you will come out as pure gold. Don't doubt God when you're in the fire and feelings of uncertainty surface. Instead, take refuge in the story of Jesus, in the book of Mark, for it shows the contradictions of how we as humans may think things should turn out once we obey God.

The beginning of Mark tells the story of John the Baptist baptizing Jesus. After Jesus is dipped in the Jordan River, the Spirit of God like a dove descends from Heaven. Suddenly a voice comes from Heaven to affirm that Jesus is the beloved Son in whom He is well pleased. In the very next verse, the scripture says the Spirit of God forced Jesus into the wilderness.

Pause!

Now, I would think that if God just affirmed that I was legit, then everything would be rainbows and unicorns, right? Wrong! Jesus was immediately put in a dry place for forty days and nights to be tempted by the devil. Thankfully, there were angels that ministered to Him continually to help Him in the journey.

I remind you of Jesus' story because it helps put things into perspective in our lives. If the Son of God, who knew who He was from birth, was put in a dry place then you can expect struggle as well. However, unlike Him, some of us struggle with our identity due to our past or current circumstances. But there is nothing—no thing—that is bigger than the plan of God for your life. Remember, you have a promise attached to your name, but you will not be able to obtain it without Christ.

I'm writing this book now because I discovered the truth of the reality. While I was not driven into a literal wilderness like Jesus, I was driven into a spiritual and emotional one. I wavered consistently back and forth between who God said I was and what my circumstances depicted. I've learned that the place of refining is a dark place, and in it rests a time of uncertainty, which happens to be the most critical space of your transition.

The great news is that God calls you by your name, the bad news is that you will not respond to it if you do not recognize it. There is a tone and the pitch of His voice that will seem foreign. You may want to run, but you must embrace it because He will not stop. Your name has favor, and we need you to fill the void in the earth that has your name on it. We need you to be who you were created to be. Yes, it is scary and you may feel unqualified, but you were destined for it. Destiny overrules qualifications set by man. Though you may know what other people have called you and the titles that have been attached to your name, whose report will you believe? I implore you to believe the report of the Lord and endure the fire, pass the test, and come out a Woman of Royalty.

Chapter Four

BEAUTIFICATION IS A SEASON OF PROCESS

"So it came about when the king's command and his decree were proclaimed and when many young women were gathered together in the citadel of Susa into the custody of Hegai, that Esther was taken to the king's palace [and placed] in the custody of Hegai, who was in charge of the women."

Esther 2:8

Sometimes we think of preparation from an individualized standpoint, which affords us the opportunity to neglect the necessary environmental preparation required. Let's think of this in the context of seasons. In the Fall season, the trees begin to shed leaves to prepare for the cold winter months. The shedding of the leaves is a signal from the atmosphere that things are changing. As humans, we look at the trees' shedding as a way of understanding that winter is coming and we should prepare wisely. Preparation may mean buying winter coats or even pulling them out of the closet. You may have to buy new things depending on where you are geographically, but you are silently preparing because you noticed the signs.

In the same way that the atmosphere begins to prepare the trees for what is to come, God prepares new environments for our arrival. Not only do you need to be ready, but the next level or arena has to be ready to receive you. With this in mind, there are large silent spaces in the book of Esther on her journey from obscurity to the palace. One reason why the Bible is silent is because of the time it took for things to be prepared. In essence, there is just as much importance in environmental preparation as there is in the individualized. Preparation is usually done in private where the individual is quiet on the matter until they have been fully readied. We see this and much more happening in this chapter.

Preparation and the Call

Esther was summoned to the royal palace with the other girls when it was decided that Queen Vashti would be replaced. There, one of the King's eunuchs gave them their beauty preparations. It is important to note that someone else administered the beauty treatments, and that the women did not put themselves through the cleansing process. Sister, this is where so many people make the dangerous mistake of attempting to make a situation better with their own might. You cannot try to make yourself beautiful on the outside when your inner man is still jacked up. If you try you will quickly see that it will not turn out well for you. A momentary fix will not help in this situation, even if it numbs the pain of your reality.

I need you to understand that there is no amount of makeup, liposuction, butt injections, or waist trainers that can do what only the spirit of God can do. God wants to give you beauty for ashes and make you into the woman He formed in your mother's womb. He wants to administer your beautification process for He knows how to get the splendor of your character out of you. He wants to dig up all the ugliness that you've acquired over the years and return to you your queenly status. You were a Queen before your first heartbreak, disappointment, and negative encounter with the world and only Jesus can restore you.

The scripture explains that Esther found favor with the eunuch Hegai who was in charge of the beauty preparations. Because of the favor she found with him, he quickly gave her the portion of beauty oils that she needed and her portion of food. Additionally, she was given seven choice maids to assist her and they were escorted to the best place in the harem. This is an important moment because Esther's process, though not completely expedited, was designed for her. She was given her portion immediately, which leads me to believe that there could have been delays for the other girls. Esther was also given the best part of the harem, which invites the understanding that there were less favorable parts. When you clock into purpose, when you move in the direction that God has for you, you will experience generally unusual levels of favor. This is why being obedient is so important because you need to be in the place where the favor will hit.

Enduring the Beautification Process

I want to use the analogy of American beauty pageants to illustrate the point of the beautification process because the pageants are a huge phenomenon that gross approximately twenty billion dollars a year. Parents of the competitors spend large sums of money for their daughters to be crowned and titled Baby Miss, Little Miss, Grand Supreme, Mini Supreme, and Queen. The young ladies spend countless hours practicing their talents, spray tanning, doing hair and makeup, and undergoing etiquette training. Have you ever watched one of those television shows where they train to become beauty queens? If so, you may have noticed that the children have to endure sometimes excruciating pain in order to prepare for the moment where they will spend time in front of judges. Sometimes the girls cry because they are tired, hungry, or irritated, and more times than not, they miss out on spending time with friends and family because of their preparation. In the same way, in order to successfully transition into your designated arena as Queen, you will have to forsake momentary fun for a greater investment. Becoming a Queen is a long-term investment, and in order to move efficaciously into your position, it requires you to be intentional about your actions and how your time is spent.

I know you're like Briana; I don't have a lot of time to invest into this process because I need to be a lot further than I already am. Can I encourage you? Anything worth having is worth fighting for. You honestly don't have the time not to invest into your process. Let's take a look at how long it took Esther: Esther 2:12 explains that,

Now when it was each young woman's turn to go before King Ahasuerus, after the end of her twelve months under the regulations for the women—for the days of their beautification were completed as follows: six months with oil of myrrh and six months with [sweet] spices and perfumes and the beauty preparations for women.

Each woman went before the King after she completed her individualized process, but not all the women completed their processes at the same time. There were so many virgins in the palace that some of them possibly waited extended periods of time until it was their turn to receive their portion. In addition to waiting until their turn came, they then had to spend an additional stint completing the twelve-month ritual. In short, they had to wait their turns. Perhaps they were anxious and wanted to expedite the process, but that didn't matter because they had an appointed time. Sister, it is important to understand that God has a set time for you to finish your preparations and you will not complete the process until you are perfected.

For the first six months, the virgins are bathed consistently with oil and myrrh. In *The Esther Anointing*, Michelle McClain-Waters explains that in ancient times myrrh was used to soften hard, dry, and cracked skin and restore its suppleness. Similarly, this is the beginning of the process where the Holy Spirit begins to chip away at that bad attitude, the idols in your life, friendships HE told you to leave alone, anger towards people, bitterness, and any other bad habits hindering Him from using you. He begins to dig you down to nothing and build you up again once He hits gold. God starts to reveal to you the truth about who you've become. Meaning, He starts to reveal those parts of you that you did not think were there. He holds a mirror up to your face and challenges you to see past the person you pretend to be. He softens your heart and beckons you to come a little closer. Honestly, God wants you to take the mask off and become the woman He created you to be, not the woman who you have become as a result of life.

My Beautification Season

When God first began to process me, I did not want to be who He was calling me to be. I just didn't want to be bothered. I was used to acting on impulse instead of what the Word of God said, and when I was coming into alignment, I had several tantrums just like the girls in the beauty pageants who have complete meltdowns when they are tired. Oftentimes the parents then have to explain to the pageant child the reasons why they must endure even when they do not want to participate. After the explanation the parents sometimes give the child a choice of continuing with the process. Sometimes the girls pull themselves together enough to participate and other times they decide that they just want to go home.

In a like manner, God also questions us in our spiritual processes. There were moments when He reminded me of the importance of my journey and bid me to trust Him in spite of my feelings. He then gave me the choice to follow Him. I'll admit that starting the beautification process stretched me because the very foundations of myself were removed from under me. I tried to stabilize in the quicksand and expended so much time and energy attempting to prevent myself from fully submitting. I wanted to be in control of my process and as a result, I learned the hard way that I was not in control. God wants us to trust Him and know that though it's painful, though you do not understand, He does and He will not let you fail. He knows the rules and guidelines of your individual pageant and He wants you to win!

I want to clarify that though the scripture states that the first six months were for oil and myrrh it does not mean that your process will only take six months. The reason that the women in Esther's time were complete with the first part of their beauty treatments during this time frame was because they were forced into the harem of the King and guarded by his eunuchs. Today, we have free will to participate or opt out of the process. Sometimes we are on board with God and sometimes we are on board with our emotions and the rest of the world. It becomes like a dance initially, one step forward and two giant steps back. But the Bible is clear that a double-minded man is unstable in all his ways (James 1:8). Therefore, in double-mindedness we can prolong our process. When this happens, be certain that God will eventually break the spirit of pride in your life that causes you to think that we are more knowledgeable than He. I have a handful of stories where I outright refused to be broken before the Lord, and there were moments where I tried to go around His instructions, only to end right back in His presence.

In retrospect, I felt like I was schizophrenic while in God's hand. One moment I decided to surrender all my cares and cast my burdens on the Lord because His yoke is easy and His burden is light (Matthew 11:30). In the next moment, I gathered those same burdens, rehearsed the situations, talked to my friends about why I hate this season, and so on. Then I would go back and declare that I trust God, but go back on the phone, get on social media, and single dating sites. The great error of logic that I have heard a couple of times is that the best way to get over a situation is by occupying your time and trying not to think about it. However, the people quoting the belief never tell you what you should be occupying your time with exactly. Should you spend time in people's DM's? Should you be on social media stalking your ex-boo that God told you to walk away from? Perhaps you may reason that you should get into another situationship to keep your mind off your pain. None of these things are helpful in the long run. What you have to do is occupy your time with the presence of God. You have to get on your face and be honest with Him because He knows how to heal you. I also want to encourage you to refrain from making life-changing decisions when your thoughts are clouding your judgment.

Guard your decisions because one day you may realize that after the pain is gone that you gave an unlikely candidate a chance. You may begin to resent them because they are not the person you need them to be, but because you "love" them you cannot leave. I put the word love in quotation marks because it may not be love that joined you two, but lust and pain instead. Sometimes people connect on the levels of their dysfunction and it can feel as intoxicating as love. I know from first-hand experience, and I do not want you to be deceived! If you heed to this warning you may save yourself from more time in the wilderness. The truth is that time does not heal all hurts, but Jesus does. I also want to warn you not to push all your emotions down and ask Jesus to heal you. Sometimes His healing method is not ours. In the past, I would pray for healing but would stop the process because I associated tears with weakness. One day, the Holy Spirit spoke to me and told me that I was stopping the healing process because I did not want to be healed the way that He chose.

I had to come to the point—and it was a very long point—that I realized that I could not keep up the toxicity of thought and action. I had to learn to surrender all and not almost. As a result of trying to hold on to things that God required I stayed in the wilderness far longer than I should have. Though my mouth said that I wanted to be free, my actions told another narrative. There was no way around the breaking. This is also a testament of God's love. He loves us so much that He will refuse to allow us to totally live beneath our calling.

In the first part of the beauty process you will be stripped of your normal dysfunction. Like gold in the fire, all of the impurities will rise to the surface. It is scary and overwhelming, yes! Running back to the familiar no matter how toxic it may have been looks glamorous. Be careful, though, because eventually you may begin to lose respect for yourself because now you know better. I want you to know that no matter how much you try to go around the process the gravitational pull will bring you right back to the place where you were. Do not prolong the time that you are taking for your beauty treatments because you have the strength to overcome any obstacle. You can change with the help of the Holy Spirit. You can do it!

Individualized Beauty Preparations

In the second half of the virgins' beautification process specifics are not given in detail. The scripture tells that the women were bathed for six months with special perfumes and ointments. Perhaps one reason why specifics are not disclosed is because each virgin was different and the preparations needed to be tailored to their body chemistry. For this reason, it is essential to realize that your journey is not going to be like the next woman's journey. Your experiences, thoughts, and expectations are unique; therefore, it is important that you do not play the comparison game. What took her one year to do might only take you five days. Ultimately, the testimony that she shares is only to encourage you, not to be used as a blueprint for your life. It is important to remember that while your lives may be similar, they are distinctly different.

Take it from me, I have played the comparison game and the results were horrible. I thought that since God introduced Jasmine to her husband within the six months into her process then He would surely do the same for me, or because I read my Bible every day and prayed every day He would speed up my process. This comparison caused me to get into the dangerous territory of seeking the hand of God instead of the face of God. I never knew what people meant by this distinction until I realized that I was performing for Him in order to get something. I was not praying to Him because He is awesome, magnificent, gracious, loving and kind, but because I was tired of sleeping in the bed alone and I wanted someone to numb my pain. You can imagine that God did not send my husband during that season but the enemy sure sent some prospects. The people who entered my life during that season sensed my pain and played into several insecurities that I had. Their presence put a Band-Aid on my wounds and when they stopped fulfilling my need of attention the wound was reopened. I believe that I also hurt them in acting as a leech by consuming their power and attention to feed a deep-seated need that had nothing to do with them.

Sister, I need you to realize that it is so important to trust that God has a unique fragrance that He wants to get out of you. The fragrance is identity specific and it only matches your body chemistry. Romans 8:11 gives the blaring reality that all of creation waits for the children of God to be revealed. How can you be revealed when you're trying to dress like Jasmine, sing like Ms. Rhoda, have your hair like Jimmy's aunty, and live like the Joneses? God wants to reveal you to the world, not the masks that you have worn over time. Think about when Adam ate the forbidden fruit in the garden of Eden. After he and Eve ate, they heard the voice of God walking through the cool of the garden and they hid out of fear. God asked Adam about His location in Genesis 3:8-9. The Lord did not ask the whereabouts of Adam because he physically hid, but because Adam became spiritually disconnected with Him. What if God is asking you the same question? Do you know where you are or when you got there? There are so many things to consider when contemplating your spiritual location, and I do not believe that you will be able to sort through your reality unless you are willing to undergo your beauty treatments to be restored. Sister, if you feel the prompting and questioning of God, it is very important that you heed to His voice.

There was a time that God asked me the very question that He asked Adam. He posed the inquiry after one of the last of many breakups with my boyfriend. Thankfully, it was in a moment when I was sober enough in my thoughts and emotions to hear Him speak. He said, "Briana, where are you?" I responded with "Here I am!" He then asked me, "Where is here?" and I didn't have an answer for that one. I was here, in a place of despair and pain, and I was literally somewhere between there and nowhere. I was lost but did not know how I got there. During this time, I literally played sermons on YouTube consecutively because I felt as if I were dying. I needed the sermons because I had neither the strength nor the energy to pull myself out of the hole I fell into. I was weak, hurting, and didn't want the help of others. I really believed that my life was over when my boyfriend and I broke up and everyday seemed to be a dark day. I wondered if I would ever recover, if I would ever get on the other side of my mountain, and if I would ever be healed. While I did not see any solution to my problem, the question that God posed to me in my weakness altered my reality as time progressed.

My individualized beauty preparations took a while to complete and there are still times when I am purged for another process. Moments ranged from rigorous cleansing and healing to more gentle moments of affirmation and love from God. There were times when I was completely separated from the people whom I loved. There were places that I was restricted from going and things that I just could not do. I felt punished a lot because it appeared that everyone else had the privilege to live their lives the way that they wanted and I could not. Secretly, I resented turning to God, but now that I am removed from the situation I'm glad that I did. I've learned that the answer is always in Christ. The healing that I sought was always in God and I desperately needed Him to save me from myself. On my beautiful journey, I've learned the advantage of completely trusting the sovereignty of God.

Hush...

"Esther did not reveal [the Jewish background of] her people or her family, for Mordecai had instructed her not to do so."

Esther 2:10

"Esther had not revealed her family or her people [that is, her Jewish background], just as Mordecai had instructed her; for Esther did what Mordecai told her just as when she was under his care."

Esther 2:20

Before Esther received her beauty preparations, she was instructed not to reveal her Jewish ancestry. While it is uncertain as to why Mordecai instructed her not to do so, it is apparent that he knew something that she did not. As the authority figure in her life, she trusted and submitted to his will, and even after she underwent her beautification treatments the scripture reiterates that Esther was still silent on the matter. We can learn from Esther's quiet and gentle spirit, and the scriptures illustrate her submission to spiritual counsel.

Spiritual counsel is not the same as natural or worldly counsel. In fact, spiritual mentors help usher you into your destiny and teach you the things of God, which demonstrates a personal investment in your growth. Similar to academic or professional mentors, spiritual mentors are the ones who have the ability to birth you into the next season of your life. They are your godly authorities that have the power to rebuke you and help bring you into alignment with the Word of God. While I did not have anyone outside of my mother embodying the role of a mentor during my process, I did listen to certain pastors and teachers from afar. The great thing is that there is no difference in the spirit and the power of technology will help to identify some limitations in our lives and will lend the ability to push past them.

I remember that there was a time during my season in the wilderness when I felt that I would never come out. I complained every chance I got and would magnify my discomfort in the season of pruning. There were lots of seesaw moments because God was cleaning out the ugly parts of me. When I had good days, I spent them worrying if tomorrow would bring more pain. When I had bad days, I would speak negative words against myself and highlight why I deserved to be in the season that I was currently living. Ultimately, I came into agreement with the thoughts that the enemy implanted into my mind and had to work harder to fall out of agreement with them. If you have done any of the things that I just mentioned, I want you to put this book down and repent. I want you to repent of your limited knowledge in this matter and every idle word you spoke in your time of pain. Sister, you cannot allow the enemy to have a field day with your emotions even though you might not feel the best about yourself. Instead of complaining and murmuring, sit before God and inquire about the path that He has for you. Ask Him to reveal to you the steps of your purpose and to give you the grace to walk out that path. Ask God to restore you.

I also challenge you to commit to taking cues from Queen Esther. She did not go to Facebook to vent about the hellishness of the beautification process, nor did she put all her business out on social media in an attempt to gain attention and sympathy from others. Instead, she closed her mouth and endured the process in private. What she learned during the beauty process carried over into her reign as Queen. If she were petty, she could have done a number of things. She could have located all the people who might have rejected her before she became Queen and rubbed her success in their face. She could have phoned her bestie and talked about how utterly stupid the guys were to reject her, but she did not. She was committed to excellence and acting like a Queen long before she received the position and even after. You have to understand that just because you arrive at a desired place does not mean that you will sustain it; therefore, your character has to be developed before you get there. If you lack good character then you may cause great harm to yourself and others.

In times of pain and less than favorable circumstances remember to hush. In reality, your complaining does not move God, but could prolong the journey. Think about the children of Israel and how it took them forty years to make an eleven-day trip. I do not know about you, but I've already wasted enough time on mindless behavior and it is time that I get to my promise land. When you begin to act like anything less than what God has called you to be then you will undergo another level of the process. Whether you like it or not, God will get what He intended out of you so it is important that you trust Him. Do not fall into the trap of complaining, gossiping, or speaking negatively over yourself. Instead, remind yourself that you are destined for Queenship and as so you shall act.

Biblical Women of Beauty

"O my love, you are altogether beautiful and fair. There is no flaw nor blemish in you!"

Song of Solomon 4:7

A quick search of the Bible reveals that compared to men there is not an abundance of information about women. However, when women are discussed they are highlighted for very important reasons. Sometimes they are identified by their infirmities, situations, or actions like the woman with the issue of blood (Luke 8:43-48), the widow and her pot of oil (2 Kings 4), or Potiphar's wife (Genesis 39). There is also the woman at the well (John 4), the Titus 2, and well-known Proverbs 31 woman who hold a substantial amount of significance in the Bible. Yet, though the women are nameless, their faith and great deeds offer important lessons to women throughout time.

With this in mind, there are seven women who are singled out for their beauty: Sarah, Rebekah, Abigail, Rachel, Abishag, Bathsheba, and Esther. Sarah was the wife of Abraham who is considered to be beautiful in appearance (Genesis 12:11). Rebekah was the wife of Abraham's brother Nahor and was very fair to look upon (Genesis 24:15). Abigail was the wife of Nabal who was a woman of good understanding and beautiful countenance (1 Samuel 25:3). Rachel who was Jacob's wife was beautiful in form and appearance (Genesis 29:17). When King David was old in age the beautiful young virgin Abishag was sought in order to help care for Him (1 Kings 1:1-4). Bathsheba was considered very beautiful in appearance (2 Samuel 11:2), and Esther was considered beautiful in form and face (Esther

2:7). Each woman though equally beautiful was noted for her beauty for various reasons. All of them were not considered to be model-like material, but some were noted as being beautiful for their wisdom and ability to help others. This leads me to believe that beauty is not just skin deep, but is largely based on the conditions of one's heart.

There are many translations of the biblical word beauty, but one interpretation is the word *tiph'ereth*, which means to have a characteristic enhancing one's appearance. Tiph'ereth is also associated with having wisdom, which is very important in making life-altering decisions. Abigail is one of the women who is noted as being beautiful and full of wisdom. A huge misconception that we have today is that certain ethnicities and physical characteristics can only be seen as beautiful. As a result, we then try to combat various limiting parameters of beauty with the phrase "beauty is in the eye of the beholder." Ok, now I understand the attempt behind that phrase and on many levels it is true; however, on deeper levels it is God's joy to give us beauty in a number of ways. It is not just physical traits that we should be concerned about, but the conditions of our heart, character, actions, and minds.

Therefore, if we look back at the women who are associated with beauty we see that Sarah, Abigail, and Esther are three women who operated in wisdom. Specifically, Sarah's ability to live by faith and birth the promised son Isaac is an amazing testament to the sovereignty of God. Strikingly, Sarah's beauty did not fade with time as we commonly think, but she aged even more beautifully as time progressed. I encourage you to take some time to read about Sarah's journey in faith. However, we must remember that though Sarah progressed beautifully she had great sorrow for she was barren. She did not have everything she wanted in the time that she desired it, and her internal defeat of barrenness caused her to make the grave decision to allow her husband to sleep with another woman. While I cannot say that I would have allowed my husband to sleep with another woman, I have seen countless women allow their husbands a "free pass" to cheat on them. My heart bleeds for those who make such decisions because if you adopt this mentality you silently believe that you are not enough to satisfy your husband. I have headline worthy news for you: YOU ARE ENOUGH! You do not have to allow someone to satisfy their lustful desires at your expense. You do not have to put yourself on sale just to have someone to talk to at night. You do not have to compromise yourself.

The Beauty of Abigail

One of my favorite women in the Bible is Abigail. While her story is not one of the most glamorous narratives it is still amazing. You can find the entire story of Nabal, David, and Abigail in 1 Samuel 25, but here is the short version: Abigail was married to a rich man named Nabal—his name means fool— who denied David's request for provisions while a fugitive in the wilderness. When David sent his men to inquire about food and shelter, Nabal pretended as if he did not know who David was. Now, it is one thing for Nabal to deny David provisions, but it is another thing to pretend that he does not have any knowledge of David. We know Nabal is pretending because he makes reference to the plight of David. Due to Nabal's insult, David decided to wage war against him vowing not to leave anyone alive and ordered two thirds of his army to prepare for battle. Fortunately, one of Nabal's men discovered David's plan and informed Abigail.

Perceiving the threat, Abigail offered David the provisions he initially requested and additional gifts as an apology. She did all of this in secret because she knew the condition of her husband's heart. Abigail had the wisdom to apologize to David and attempt to diffuse the situation before he killed her husband and all of his men. She did not go and pop off at the mouth to her husband, nor did she degrade him in front of other people, but she moved in silence and pled for his life.

I want you to notice the posture of Abigail. She did not fuel an already simmering fire but she shows humility and reverence to David. In turn, David identifies her as a woman of discretion and discernment. This is the heart posture that God seeks to get out of us. We are to act as intercessors in the earth to pray for others and shift atmospheres. Abigail could have easily gone to her husband and got an attitude and allowed him to learn his lesson. Unfortunately, his lesson would have been the tragedy of death, but out of love she went secretly to David and attempted to lessen the blow. Not only did she apologize for her husband, but she took on the blame. Women we must practice the ways of Abigail and take our cares to the Lord. We will not win battles with our attitudes, our negative words or the bad logics that we have picked up along the way. Instead, we have to humble ourselves and pray for the people in our lives.

Shortly after the ordeal with David, Abigail's husband died and she was left uncovered, but guess what happens? She becomes the wife of David and steps into an arena of royalty. What if Abigail decided to let the chips fall where they may?

Do you think David would have taken her as a wife? Probably not. Through her wisdom and ability to intercede for others she was granted to reward of becoming a wife of the future King.

In essence, during the beautification process, the Lord has to snatch up old roots that lay dormant in your life. Ultimately, He has to deprogram the toxic feelings and mentalities that you have picked up along the way. You may also begin to realize how much you bought into the ideologies of other people when they start to surface in your actions. Ultimately, you have to deal with the hidden things in your life when God reveals them to you. In every season you must obey but especially in this season. It is scary, I know, but it is worth the pain.

Chapter Five

CROWNING DAY

"So Esther was taken to King Ahasuerus, to his royal palace in the tenth month, that is, the month of Tebeth (Dec-Jan), in the seventh year of his reign. Now the king loved Esther more than all the other women, and she found favor and kindness with him more than all the [other] virgins, so that he set the royal crown on her head and made her queen in the place of Vashti."

Esther 2:16-17

E sther has been in God's training camp until this point. She has been stretched, tested, proven, and we see that her will has been broken even in the face of fear because she realized the call on her life. There were people waiting on her to fulfill her destiny as millions of lives depended on her choosing rightly. I do not want to be presumptuous and assume that Esther endured her process with ease, but I think she knew that there is beauty at the other end of the tunnel. Esther did not allow her hesitation, past, or age to deter her from being a bold woman. Like many of us, she had to overcome the small voices in her head betting against her destiny. Ultimately, to win the war in the mind is the first victory, but it's no small feat.

So many times we vacillate over the position without realizing the weight required to maintain. We become wrapped up in the applause that we neglect to account for the behind the scenes feelings of inadequacy and self-denial. It is interesting that at any given time it can be the best of times and the worst of times at the same time. Becoming a Queen is hard work, and sustaining the position is even more tenuous. Yet, we will adapt to the necessary pressures of life when we get into the destiny groove.

The virgins went before the King with anything that would elevate their beauty after the beautification process. They would go in the evening and leave in the morning, but when they left the King they were escorted to the second harem where his concubines were held. There, they awaited their fate possibly hoping that the King would favor them. Unfortunately, unless he delighted in the young woman and called her by name she could not return to him. The name that the King would call is the same name that we spoke about in a previous chapter that has favor attached for a particular purpose.

Esther was still required to wait until her appointed time though she completed her process within a year. The scripture explains that Esther was taken to the King in the tenth month, which was the seventh year of his reign. Let's look at the timeframe leading up to Esther's crowning. The initial feast with Vashti happened in the third year of the King's reign

(Esther 1:3), and virgins were sought between the third and sixth year. Esther enters the palace in the seventh year for her beauty treatments, which were done in the same year due to the favor she found with the eunuch. After the treatments were completed she went for her night with the King in the tenth month of the seventh year of his kingship (Esther 2:16-17), which is after one year of beauty treatments and ten months of waiting. Therefore, Esther waited and prepared for almost two years for her night to win an audience with the King. By faith, Esther walked blindly into the private room of the King and she was favored.

I can only imagine the level of fear that operated in Esther. After all, she was in her early teens when she went to the King's bed. I do not see how she could have been confident in her night with him because he was an experienced adult and she was not. He was a man who had prior history with women and that could be intimidating. However, she went when she was called no matter how frightening the situation. Similarly, when God calls us into our royal arena we may experience comparable feelings as Esther. We may not feel qualified and think that someone else can do the job better, but if God wanted other people to fulfill your destiny He would have called them. It is important that you remind yourself that it is you who He wants to bring the glory to Him. It is your fragrance that the world needs.

Returning back to the scriptures, there was a banquet thrown in Esther's honor after she was crowned. Now this is an event that solidified her place in the palace and we would think that everything was over, right? She was Queen after all! Well, yes she was Queen, but she had to endure another process. Esther was crowned Queen in chapter 2 verse 17, but she is not referred to as a Queen by the narrator of the book until verse 22, and not verbally acknowledged by the King as such in the scripture until chapter 5. God is showing us something very important here. There is a reason as to why there are lapses in time before the King acknowledges Esther as Queen, and why her position is understood long before she seems to embody it. Through the silences in the scripture, we can see that Esther still needed character development to fully embody the role she was given. Just because she had the title of Queen does not mean that she was such in practice, character, and spirit. I want to caution you to be careful not to judge a place as having made it if your personhood cannot sustain you because the title can be stripped from you.

Embodying Your Position

I'm sure Esther was beautiful when she was crowned in the seventh year of the King's reign; however, it is difficult to ignore the time between when she was crowned and recognized as Queen. In fact, it is not until after the twelfth year of King Ahasuerus' reign that he calls her by her titled position. On the one hand, the scripture shows us that after Esther was crowned, the King coordinated a party in her honor called "Esther's Banquet." On the other hand, however, the title of Queen is missing. And, though the narrator of the story acknowledges Esther as crowned and the people who are around her know that she is, it is still not expressed from the mouths of people. The reason is because Esther had to grow into her position. Just because she had all the physical manifestations of a Queen does not mean that she was the quintessence of one.

There will be times when God calls you to do something and you feel unqualified. You may also reason that someone else is better for the job than you. When you have those moments of doubt you have to remember that if God wanted the other person to do it he would have appointed them and not you. Can you look back over your life and see any moment where you were tasked to do something but didn't because you were fearful? Maybe you did do it but you sabotaged the opportunity. Esther was in the same position but on another level. She gained Queenship based on the favor of God at birth and earned it with the eunuch when she was in her teenage years, but she still had to grow into the manifestation of a responsible woman before she could be acknowledged as such.

The good news is that God recognized Esther as Queen though she did not. If we imagine the voice of the writer of the book of Esther as God then we can see how He thinks of her. In various parts of the scripture, Esther is written as Queen between crowning day and the King's vocalization. In the same vein, God has written something about you and is calling you from an elevated position. You are a Queen though your actions may not seamlessly align with Queenly behavior. You are a Queen though your circumstances are less favorable. You are still a Queen even if you had an abortion, miscarriage, sex out of wedlock, or are currently shacking up. God will call you to higher heights and His call will be so elevated that it will cause you to become as such. Granted, this process takes time but it is so worth it!

Your Character Effectively Sustains Your Destiny

"But the plot became known to Mordecai, who informed Queen Esther, and Esther told the king in Mordecai's name."

Esther 2:22

One development in the process of becoming a Woman of Royalty is establishing good character. One reason why Esther was not immediately called Queen is because she was not ready spiritually, emotionally, or characteristically. In fact, she was put into a position directly after her cleansing process. While the beautification process stripped her of the impurities that she was carrying, her immune system, so to speak, was not built high enough to sustain her new environment. Therefore, she underwent another process to develop the character that would sustain her in the palace.

During Esther's reign her cousin Mordecai discovered that two of the King's eunuch were plotting to attack him and informed her. Esther relayed the message and after an investigation the eunuchs were punished and hung from the gallows. Honestly, Esther's association with Mordecai saved the King's life. Therefore, her positioning in the kingdom was not only for her benefit but for the benefit of others as well. Her positioning allowed her to give the message to the King immediately to assure his health and safety of the palace.

Notice the scripture says that Esther gave credit to Mordecai for having found out the matter. Esther did not pretend to be the one who discovered the evil plot nor did she use the information to advance her favor with the King. Instead, she diverted the attention off of her and gave credit where credit was due. She did not pose as a hater, or someone who threw shade because the information came back as true. Instead, Esther gave Mordecai what he rightfully deserved.

Have you ever struggled with doing what Esther did? I know I have wrestled with someone else getting noticed, and struggled with envy and covetousness. In fact, my lack of security caused me to be an undercover hater who disliked people for no reason. Over time, I have found that the area of our insecurity will highlight the posture of our heart. There are certain areas where I am not as strong but I would judge other people who were strong in the area of my weakness. Subconsciously, I became jealous of those people just because they possessed a quality that I wished to have. Looking back, it amazes me how jealousy is rationalized. If we see a woman who we perceive as less than desirable with a handsome man, we might say that she had to have gotten him when he did not have anything. Or, we coach ourselves into believing that she had to do "a lot" to score a man like that. Or, here is my favorite: "I know if she can get a man, I definitely can get one." Does any of that ring familiar for you? If so, you have to work on your character because you are envying her because she has something that you secretly desire.

If you agree with anything I said above then you have to allow God to work on your heart, which will transform your character. I once heard a speaker say that you cannot go where your character will not sustain you and I find this to be true in so many areas. Unfortunately, people do not have the heart or the character for their position, but out of the human need for recognition and authority we stay in these positions no matter what. Lady, be careful not to cause yourself unnecessary pain by attempting to perform a duty that is not designed for you.

You should not do something to maliciously outshine another person. If you are walking in destiny and on purpose then your light will shine automatically.

Responsibility Does NOT Stop with You

"Go, gather all the Jews that are present in Susa, and observe a fast for me; do not eat or drink for three days, night or day. I and my maids also will fast in the same way. Then I will go in to [see] the king [without being summoned], which is against the law; and if I perish, I perish."

Esther 4:16 (Emphasis Added)

On the surface, Esther became Queen because the King was searching for a woman to replace Vashti. However, on deeper levels she was crowned because God called her to be a voice in the earth to save His people. A few years into Esther's Queenship the King appointed Haman, who is identified as the enemy of the Jews, to a very high position in the kingdom. Haman was the most powerful official in the entire empire. As a result of his new positon, the King commanded that everyone bow to Haman every time he passed. However, one man did not bow and his name was Mordecai. Yes, Esther's cousin refused to bow to man because he served God.

You can imagine how many issues this caused. If the King's advisors felt that all the women would begin to dishonor their husbands if Vashti was let off the hook, imagine what would happen if one man were permitted not to bow. Something had to be done to teach Mordecai a lesson and Haman set out to massacre not only him, but every other Jew in the land. Now, the scripture does not say that Haman was an enemy of

Mordecai, but an enemy of the Jews, which signals a long history of discord.

Scripture reveals that when Mordecai found out about Haman's plan he was very vexed, and I am sure fear gripped his heart. Have you ever gotten some news that made your heart drop? I am speaking about that gut wrenching feeling that sickens you and strips you of your appetite. This was Mordecai's state of mind because he tore his clothes, covered himself in ashes, and went into the city to cry aloud. The rest of the Jews in the land wailed also when they heard of the King's signed decree. Collectively they fasted, wept, covered themselves in ashes, and wore sack clothes, which is a traditional sign of mourning.

When Esther heard that her cousin was in mourning she sought the cause. Mordecai relayed the plan of Haman and the King's given permission to kill, slaughter, and annihilate the Jews. While Esther was compelled to intervene because of her Jewish ancestry, the fear of the law initially staggered her actions. Armed with the knowledge of what would be done to the Jews and asked to contend on their behalf by Mordecai, Esther offers an excuse in Esther 4:11:

All the king's servants and the people of the king's provinces know that for any man or woman who comes to the king to the inner court without being summoned, he has but one law, that he is to be put to death, unless the king holds out to him the golden scepter so that he may live. And as for me, I have not been summoned to come to the king for these [last] thirty days.

Esther struggles when asked to rise to a higher occasion. She points out that the King's officials and residents know that death is their portion if they go unsummoned to the King. She attempts to explain to Mordecai that though she is in a high position, even she, who has favor with the King may not be spared. Esther is in legitimate fear of her life and no one can blame her. Sometimes God can call us to do something that might cause adversity in our lives. Maybe it is not something that you might lose your life over, but you may lose your reputation, job, peace, or family. This is even true in the romantic relationships that the Lord might tell you to leave, or have told you to leave a long time ago, but the silence of being alone is so deafening that you refused.

In essence, God will put you in positions of grace that will carry you to higher levels, but He will also require something of you that you want to keep. He wants to know that you love Him more than worldly things. He wants to know that even if He cuts you that you will still praise Him. He wants to know if you love Him or His gifts more. God wants you to lay your life down for His cause. Luke 12:48, the latter portion of the verse reminds us that to whom much is given much is required. Do you know that God will always requires much? We can replace the word much and insert something that you held dearly that He wanted. I know when the Lord required my much it took me six years to fully give it to Him. This means he asked for it in 2010 and I did not let it go until 2016 and even then I still held on to parts of it. You can imagine the agony I went through in those years attempting to keep alive something that God killed. I caused a lot of harm to myself and learned that the reason why self-inflicted wounds are so ugly is because they represent the reality that we turned against ourselves. Fear can do that to us.

Esther's fear rested in the reality that she had to make a decision that could punish her to death. Yes, she was Queen. Yes, she won favor. Yes, she is in the palace and is knowledgeable about how the kingdom operates, but she was still fearful. On the other hand, I want to remind you that,

> God did not give us a spirit of timidity or cowardice or fear, but [He has given us a spirit] of power and of love and of sound judgment and personal discipline [abilities that result in a calm, well-balanced mind and self-control]. (2 Timothy 1:7)

The enemy will always attack you with a form of fear in order to prevent you from doing the will of God. Fear can be described as False Evidence Appearing Real. An understanding of the acronym is a blessing because while the law of the land may say one thing, the Word of God says another. His law, His Word, and His advice trump what man has put in place concerning morals, character, and decision making. In the same way, though Esther was a Jew, her internal view was even more blurred when she entered into the kingdom.

So far, we have yet to see Esther completely embody who she is as a child of God and a woman of stature. So, when she reminds Mordecai of the law of the land, she does so as to not put herself in harm's way. Maybe Esther felt like an impostor. Maybe she thought that she was insignificant because of the way she obtained her role. Whatever her reasoning, it is clear that she did not feel set apart from other people. On the other hand, Esther's response to Mordecai has undertones that allude to the belief that her Queenly title would protect her from the massacre of Haman. Understandably, Esther wanted to preserve her life and the fight or flight instinct definitely kicked in, but Mordecai's response to her is sobering as he tells her:

> *Do not imagine that you in the king's palace can escape any more than all the Jews. For if you remain silent at this time, liberation and rescue will arise for the Jews from another place, and you and your father's house will perish [since you did not help when you had the chance]. And who knows whether you have attained royalty for such a time as this [and for this very purpose]?" (Esther 4:13-14)*

Basically, he pulls Esther's "safety" card because she forgot where she came from. He tells her that she will not escape judgment just because she is in the palace. He reminds her that she is still Jewish and cannot hide from this horrible reality because she will eventually suffer like everyone else. Mordecai challenges her to speak up and intervene for what is right. He calls her out of hiding and imparts destiny to her in the form of a question, "Who knows if perhaps you were made Queen for such a time as this?"

The amazing thing to me is that Esther attempts to disassociate herself from the very people she is called to. The Jews have the same proclivities and fears that she does, but since she has moved into a place of prominence, she tries to disconnect with that part of her identity. However, it is the very part that she attempts to remove that saves her. She is called to save the people with whom she can identify.

It is interesting the amount of fervency that people fight with to save those who have their same infirmity. I have a heart for women who struggle with self-esteem and identity issues, the very women who may have settled in the place of their dysfunction, but have the will to move higher. The reason I have the heart for these women is because I was once among them. I know their struggles, their thought processes, their pain, which is why God saved me to deliver them since I am one from among them.

It is important that I explain to you that when God sends someone in your life to speak to your destiny, it will generally cause you to change. I can attest to this truth on several occasions in my life. God would speak a word into my life and tell me that I would have great things, but my current circumstances would defy what he said. Yet, slowly but surely things would begin to manifest and align with what he said about me, and when I set my heart to believe I was also changed and aligned with His will over my life. Surely, change comes from within and moves outwardly, and a changed mind manifests in changed actions.

When Esther receives Mordecai's correction she makes a decision to change. She decides to sacrifice her life because she knows that the assignment is bigger than her comfort. She requests that the Jews fast and pray with her in preparation for her task. We witness her will coming into alignment with her assignment as she resolves her former resistance in the statement, "If I perish, I perish." Sometimes when we are reading we take the words on the page for granted. Yet, I love the *if* in her statement because it shows that while things have been historically one way there is hope that there will be a different outcome because she is sent by God. Esther's hope is in God alone and she becomes solely dependent on Him, which is further signified by her fast later in the chapter.

The King refers to Esther as Queen in the next chapter and not a moment before. Esther had to mature into the role of

Queen, and had to be willing to do what was right whether it cost comfort or her life. She took on the responsibility of saving others, living a sacrificial life, and finally truly became Queen.

Chapter Six

CALLED TO TAKE A STAND

"In all your ways know and acknowledge and recognize Him, And He will make your paths straight and smooth [removing obstacles that block your way]."

Proverbs 3:6

In the previous chapter, we talked about how Esther was tasked to make a difference in the lives of her people by pleading on their behalf. She made a decision to push past the fear that initially surfaced in her life. Like Esther, when the Lord asks us to do something we may be initially afraid because we may not know the cost or outcome. Unfortunately, for many people, the fear of failure or success stops them from doing many things that they have been graced to do.

Moving back to the latter part of Mordecai's response to Esther in chapter 5, he asks her how does she know that she did not "attain royalty for such a time as this?" The word royalty is mentioned for the first time in the scripture and though royal was previously mentioned, theologians agree that the law of first mention is important because it sets the precedence for everything that will follow. While the law of first mention is generally geared towards the first time it is mentioned in the entire Bible, I think it is equally important to apply such an understanding to when it is mentioned for the first time in a book as well.

Thinking about Mordecai's words made me realize that he did not only correct Esther, but he spoke awareness into her life. He stopped speaking to her fears and uncertainties, and spoke to who she was in the physical as well as who she was destined to become. Without a doubt, he spoke to her royal status in the eyes of God and man, and called that from within her. Mordecai spoke to her secret dwelling place, which canceled her ability to rest in fear.

Destiny Actions Have a Language

"Go, gather all the Jews that are present in Susa, and observe a fast for me; do not eat or drink for three days, night or day. I and my maids also will fast in the same way. Then I will go in to [see] the king [without being summoned], which is against the law; and if I perish, I perish."

Esther 4:16

We saw in the previous chapter that Esther gave every honorable excuse as to why she could not intercede on the Jews' behalf. I can imagine the inner pain she experienced while contemplating Mordecai's request. She may have wondered how she could do it and where the courage would come from. Perhaps she wrecked her mind trying to figure out if the King still favored her. These are questions and many more she possibly had as she contemplated her assignment.

However, Mordecai put a demand on her future not her present. Ultimately, he spoke in a language that she recognized subconsciously. Yes, she was Queen, but did God appoint her to this position for such a time as this? Was this truly her destiny even though she was still in the palace? In the end, Esther decided to bear the weight of the command and responded with obedience, which challenged the life she once lived. It is interesting that in spite of being an orphan and a victim of sex trafficking, Esther wanted to hold on to her life. This mentality is also applicable to the ways in which we hold on to our dysfunction even if we are given the opportunity to have something better. Unfortunately, many of us do not make it to the point of Esther because we are unwilling to let go of our corrupt systems to push into the new.

Nevertheless, Esther knew that she could not carry through with this plan without the help of God. Understandably, in her strength she was aware that she could not move the King. After all, she was disobeying his laws by going to see him unsummoned, but God gave her the victory! We see that Esther believed in the power of the Lord who has the ability and capability to turn the hearts of people in whatever way He wants. Because of her dependence on God, she asked the Jews to fast with her so that everyone would be in agreement. If it were the will of God for her to occupy this position for such a time as this, then fasting to fully align with His purpose would give her a certain sense of security. We see that Esther responded to the language of her destiny with dignity and grace, and she rejected her will for one that was greater than hers. Again, she had to walk by faith and not by sight, which is an action that further aligns her with Sarah as a woman of faith who was considered beautiful.

The Power of Fasting

Women of Royalty know the power of fasting. I would also go as far as to say that it is impossible to fulfill the plan of God for your life without it. Among other things, fasting humbles us, purifies our faith, brings spiritual insight, and makes room for the Holy Spirit. Over time, I have learned the power of fasting when there were moments where I needed to hear from God. In other words, fasting is an act of denying your flesh for spiritual reasons. It is an uncomfortable action, and you may feel like you cannot make it but you can.

I am a witness that the flesh will lead you into situations where you do not want to be and keep you there longer than you wish to stay. I've stayed in plenty of dead relationships because of an active sexual soul tie. Though I knew the relationships were killing me, it was like my feet were stuck in cement that wouldn't allow me to move. However, over time if you keep trying and stay diligent, you will learn just how much discipline starts with a decision. You will begin to understand the art of delayed gratification because it will make a major difference in your decision-making.

Now I want to be clear and let you know that a simple decision will not be your saving grace, but it is a start. It is essential that you partner with the power of the Holy Spirit to endure and sustain this lifestyle change if you hope to be victorious. You have to develop the habit of asking God for the grace to move in the direction that He is leading you. This is also a practice that should be used in fasting. When you fast you bring your will and flesh under subjection of the Lord. Fasting is undeniably a warfare strategy that requires and demands humbleness. One benefit of practicing fasting actively is that your spiritual senses are sharpened in a way that allows you to tap into a power that you would not normally have.

Tsôwn is the word for fast in Hebrew and it means to cover the mouth. In the same way that food nourishes and strengthens our bodies, the Word of God is our spiritual nourishment that has everlasting impacts. For example, while on a 40-day fast in the wilderness, Satan tempts Jesus and He rebukes Satan by repeating the Word of God: "It is written and forever remains written, 'Man shall not live by bread alone, but by every word that comes out of the mouth of God'" (Matthew 4:4). Now that is a powerful statement because it exposes the fact that if we ever hope to have the victory then we have to learn to chew on the Word of Life. If Jesus did not know the Word of God then He may have lost the battle. Unfortunately, so many times people pay attention to their physical conditions, but neglect their spiritual health and are left unbalanced. When we favor our physical conditions over our spiritual ones then we are losing the battle with the enemy in more ways than one. However, when fasting we break the ties with the physical world as we rely solely on that of the spiritual realm to be sustained.

I want you to think of fasting as a way to gain insight and strength you did not originally have. Some reasons why many do not fast are because they either do not know how, or they have the wrong perception of it. If we approach fasting from the standpoint of the things we are denying ourselves of then we will not do it successfully, but when we approach it from the stance of what we are gaining we will have the victory every time.

We also have to be aware of the fact that we have an enemy who wants to destroy us. Our enemy is Satan, the devil! Can you imagine why he wants to destroy us, or why he works so hard to discredit us? I will explain it to you this way, Lucifer was kicked out of heaven and took a third of the angels with him; however, his being kicked out is not the only reason that he is upset. The fact that he disobeyed God once and was punished for eternity is why he is mad. Yet, when we disobey God, He shows His love to us, extends grace and mercy as He forgives us. We are even seated in heavenly places with the Father (Ephesians 2:6). So, the devil is jealous and angry that God gives us redemptive chances and even sent His son to die for us. The devil works tirelessly to keep us bound and out of the will of God, and is miserable because he has already been defeated.

When I first started fasting, I started with one day because I did not want to do it wrong. In this case, I believe that Lord led me to start this way because He was training me for longer periods of time. Over time, I have been able to build endurance and grow stronger while learning how to discipline my flesh to obey the Word. Ladies please remember that this journey is a marathon and not a race. God wants you to grow with Him and it is essential to recognize that you should not fast in your own power. It takes the power of God to successfully fast and you do not have to try to be a super Christian and go on a fast like

Jesus for 40 days. But, pray that God lead you on the type of fast He wants and that He will help you sustain it.

Esther's Fast

Esther commanded that all of the Jews enter into corporate fasting for three days and three nights. The Jews were in crisis and they needed God to intercede on their behalf. This is also the first time we see Esther take a stand for anything! This is the moment when she actually found herself. She called the fast because she realized that she had come to the end of herself and needed the assistance of God.

In Esther's time of fasting she sought God because she knew that her title meant absolutely nothing. She needed direction and divine strategy. Notice that she still did not have an overly optimistic attitude. Though she called the fast, the possibility of dying was still intertwined with her thoughts. On one hand, her command to the Jews is noble and shows great responsibility. On the other hand, it still highlights her human reasoning and fear. In fact, this is the second time she reminds Mordecai of the potential consequences of her going against the King's rules. How many times do we remind others, ourselves, or God about our circumstances? How many times do we make excuses to not do something? Here is why we need to fast because it helps us gain heavenly perspective and weakens the voice of the flesh that wants to preserve itself.

During your time of fasting, you may not immediately feel like everything will be ok, especially on the first day. Your flesh will be loud, you may be grumpy and even physically weak, but you have to remind yourself that man does not live by bread alone, but every word that proceeds out of the mouth of God

(Matthew 4:4). I want to encourage you to keep pushing through this time and ask the Holy Spirit to help you. Unfortunately, many people do not know the Holy Spirit. Some might think He is an "it," but He is a person. In fact, Jesus reminds us that He is the comforter. The Holy Spirit is part of the Godhead—Father, Spirit, and Son—and is working through us. He is not one to be feared because He is full of love and assistance. I talk and call on Him often because when I fast I cannot depend on myself for anything.

I have noticed that I feel a sense of peace when I come out of the three day fast. No, the situation may not change and the obstacles still may be present but I am eased. I believe that during this time I cast my cares on the Lord and relinquish my will for His. My posture of fasting is a sign to God that I do not have it all together and I would fail miserably without Him. I've learned that it gives God great joy to provide for His children because He delights in us, but so many of us have difficulty with trusting Him because people have let us down in the past. Overwhelmingly, our past experiences make it hard to believe in Him because we have been so traumatized by humans. However, God is not like inconsistent people here on earth. I am reminded of what Numbers 23:19 says,

> *God is not a man, that He should lie, Nor a son of man, that He should repent. Has He said, and will He not do it? Or has He spoken and will He not make it good and fulfill it?*

It does not say that God will not lie but that He cannot lie. If He said something, then He will bring it to pass, but many of us are not listening because we are busy nursing our hurts. Please do not nurture the pain of your past over the freedom of your future. I want you to honestly ask yourself if you can hear as well as you think. Perhaps you can hear, but are you listening? Contrary to popular belief, the art of listening requires action and if you have any doubt then you have to begin to train your ear to hear the spiritual conversations going on in the heavens.

After Esther's fast, the Bible tells us that she put on her garments and went in before the King unsummoned. It is apparent that she had a strategy in latter chapters, but it could not have been done without the Lord. God gave her divine instructions that would not only secure her safety, but the safety of the Jews as well. Therefore, I encourage you to practice turning your plate down before making life-changing decisions. See what the Father has to say before you prematurely get into a relationship, take a new job, or anything that may alter the path of your destiny because Women of Royalty live a life of prayer and fasting!

Chapter Seven

ROYAL GARMENTS

"On the third day [of the fast] Esther put on her royal robes and stood in the inner court of the king's palace opposite his [throne] room. The king was sitting on his royal throne, facing the [main] entrance of the palace."

Esther 5:1

E sther got up and put on her clothes after the corporate fast. She went to the King after she spent time seeking the face of God, praying for His guidance and favor, and even His strategy. Before this point her royal garments aren't mentioned. Not even when she is crowned Queen is there any discussion of her attire. While she may have worn them before, the scripture only mentions them after the fast. I believe that the royal garments are mentioned because Esther completed the prerequisite to become a Woman of Royalty. She was obedient, she accepted her position, she fasted, prayed, and she submitted herself unto the Lord. Through the process, Esther grew into her positioning as Queen and thus her destiny. She could now embody the position with confidence. She has trained her ear to hear the voice of God and waited on His timing. In short, Esther pleased God and He cleared her to move into the next phase of her destiny.

Gratefully, Esther did not make a hasty decision to just go to the King without being led by God. She took her queue from the Creator and executed her plan with grace, dignity and precaution. Though Esther put on physical robes that were befitting for a Queen, she also showcases how stunning spiritual robes are. Her actions for the remainder of the story demonstrate how important it is for a woman of royalty to be fully clothed in royal attire. Our robes must match the place that we are entering. Esther was going to the King who was sitting on a royal throne and could not go in his presence unprepared or ill-dressed. Her clothing had to match the place of her next footing, and in positioning herself accordingly she reached the place of destiny.

Positioning, Patience, and Humility

"When the king saw Esther the queen standing in the court, she found favor in his sight; and the king extended to her the golden scepter which was in his hand. So Esther approached and touched the top of the scepter."

Esther 5:2

She did not immediately go to the King anxious and irate when she entered the royal court. Instead she used those moments to spend more time with the Father in order to allow Him to speak through her when she was acknowledged. The Scripture tells us that Esther once again found favor in the King's sight when he saw her waiting. I wonder how long Esther was standing there. Was it one minute? Five minutes? More? We do not know, but when the King saw her she found favor. Esther stood patiently.

Ladies, when we are waiting on God to send our spouse, promotion, or even healing, it is easy to get antsy. We want certain things quickly and by any means necessary. Yet, there is a risk in attempting to rush the hand of God. There have been countless times when I became impatient and tried to take matters in my own hands, and each time I ended up flat on my back crying out the Father for forgiveness and mercy. I want to warn you of the excruciating pain associated with overriding the Holy Spirit because it can cost you a lot. It is okay to trust God to bring whatever you need in His timing because it is always perfect.

There is also a possibility that we can be positioned physically where we are not spiritually. This is an Ouch moment! There are times where we are given something but cannot sustain it. There are also times that we may find ourselves in compromisingly bad situations after we planned to stay on a straight and narrow path. Yet, unless we partner with God and do the spiritual work of aligning our will with His then we will fail. Do not get me wrong and think that physical placement is not important, because it is; but, we will not be able to stay in the place if we are not spiritually ready.

One reason why the Bible does not give a specific time for how long Esther stood in the court before the King noticed her is because of our proclivity to measure ourselves by other people. Getting in position does not mean that God will immediately flip the spot light switch, but your positioning is vital to your purpose and there still may be things that need to be worked out inside of you. With this in mind, Esther waited for the King to call her as she introspectively surveyed herself. It is quite possible that Esther still had a bit of nervousness in her spirit because she was breaking the law. She could have even given herself a pep talk in order to speak to the fear welling inside her body, but despite the uncertainty she walked by faith and not by sight.

Due to her total dependence on God she found favor in the King's sight. There is a difference between having the ability to see and being in someone's sight. Though majority of the time we use these words interchangeably, they are not the same and the collapsing of the two diminishes the value of the other. For example, one day I went to the optometrist for an eye exam for glasses. Though I have worn glasses and/or contacts for quite some time, I needed to get my eyes checked. There were signs that I needed new glasses such as frequent headaches, straining to see in the distance, and blurring of words. When the optometrist examined my eyes she told me that they were in perfect health; however, I needed a stronger prescription because the astigmatism in both eyes worsened. An astigmatism in the eye means that the front surface of the eye is not curved properly so when light rays enter they do not focus accurately on the retina that results in blurred vision. While I still can see, my sight is not as perfect as it could be and the flaw in my vision can cause me to misinterpret images. Not having clear enough vision could potentially put others in danger as well. Needless to say, I received a new prescription for glasses—which aid me in seeing more clearly—and my sight is amazing.

In the same manner, God metaphorically poses as glasses for the King to help Him perceive Esther correctly. I am sure the King remembered his law that forbade anyone to come into his presence unsummoned, but when he noticed Esther, when he saw her clearly for who she was, she found favor in his sight. (In)sight is the ability to gain a deeper understanding of a person or a thing. I am sure that God imparted awareness into the King about her so that she could accomplish His will for her life. Insight comes from knowledge whether the source is recognized or not. When we gain a deeper understanding of how something works or why someone acts a certain way many times our perspective changes about them. In a like manner, behind the scenes, God ensured a safe environment for Esther.

Another characteristic that Esther showed even after she gained favor with the King is humility. The Bible tells that she touches the top of the scepter. The act of touching the scepter shows Esther's respect for the King's position. It is essential that she move in reverence when he points his scepter to grant Esther permission to approach him. Humility and reverence are key characteristics to have if God is going to elevate you. Be sure that if ungodly characteristics start to surface, you will be cut back in order to be pruned. Let's take some cues from Queen Esther just to be safe!

You might be thinking "but Esther was a Queen and I am not." While this is true according to social recognition, there are two sides to every story. In the times of Esther, the Queen did not have as much say or ruling power as we might think. Ultimately, she was the woman who was at the beck and call of the King, and had to do everything he asked of her if she wished to keep her position. Therefore, Esther could not make major decisions without the King's approval and he ruled over her just like he did the common people.

Try to think back to times in your life where you felt like something or someone was controlling you. Maybe you fell ill and could not make major decisions concerning your health. Perhaps you had a soul tie that you could not break and it controlled your emotions. You may have been hurt in the past so much so that it impacted the way you relate today. These external controlling factors are real! Though they may not necessarily be dictators in your life, they do have the capacity to limit you in some way. To put it plain, Queen Esther was a high level servant of the King who didn't have control over her own body. Even more, when Mordecai made a request of her to intercede for the Jews she had not been seen the King in 30 days. Talk about marriage! But, this shows that Esther was not in a particularly favorable position, but in a position of purpose and humility that turned out for her good.

Turning the lens back to the personal, the more time we spend with God the more He will expose the hindering aspects within us. This is truly a humbling experience and I have had countless crying sessions on the couch with the Holy Spirit because of the truth about myself. The discovery of some of my issues caused real humility to bubble over in my life. I am referring to the blaring awareness that we are not worthy and no matter how hard we work or how awesome we think we are. Neighboring on this, the Bible tells us that even on our best days we are not righteous (Romans 3:10). Yet, the common misconception is that if you are a good person then bad things will not happen, or that being a good person will exempt people from the chastisement of God. I disagree with this thinking because bad things happen to good people all the time. And, being considered "good" is relative and a bit dangerous. In Romans 12:3 the Bible tells us,

> For by the grace [of God] given to me I say to everyone of you not to think more highly of Himself [and of His importance and ability] than he ought to think; but to think so as to have sound judgment, as God has apportioned to each a degree of faith [and a purpose designed for service].

The scripture illuminates the truth that we cannot judge others or ourselves by ourselves. Instead, we must compare all flesh to Christ and His perfection. If we do that, we have a greater chance of keeping in line with patience and humility.

Slow to Speak

Esther proceeded silently when the King extended his scepter as acknowledgement of her acceptance. Her actions are important because sometimes our need to be heard can get in the way of the progress we want. Sometimes we start to over talk and under listen, as we feel that what we have to say is more important than others' opinions. Esther realized the importance of silence and she won half the battle long before she made her needs known unto the King. When you are slow to speak you are displaying wisdom. When you are in a tough situation and making a life changing decision, stop and wait on God. Sometimes we get nervous and want a rushed answer and result, but are upset when we do not receive the response that we are seeking. I believe that the reaction of hastening is a direct result of unsettlement from within. One reason that Esther proceeded the way she did is because she spent time with God and was able to humble herself before the King and act according to His divine strategy. I agree with the folklore proverb that says, "You catch more bees with honey!" The biblical translation of this common phrase is Proverbs 15:1,

> *A soft and gentle and thoughtful answer turns away wrath,*
> *But harsh and painful and careless words stir up anger.*

The proof of the truth of the scripture is in the next verse of Esther.

Before Esther made her request known to the King, he asked her a question and immediately offered her a solution. In chapter 5, just moments after Esther touches the scepter the King asks about the reason for her visit. He asks,

> *What is troubling you, Queen Esther? What is your request?*
> *It shall be given to you, up to half of the kingdom.*

It is amazing how she is offered even more than that which she was going to ask. Ultimately, we see the King questioning her desire. He did not ask what she needed today, but he asks about her long term longing. The word desire means to want or wish for something. It is important to understand that a desire and a need are two different things and they hold two different weights. The King is inquiring about her wants and wishes and though he perceives her as wanting something he does not fully realize the level of her need.

Though his surface level perceptions are correct, he offers her material things as a solution. Unfortunately, the material solution is not enough for an emotional and spiritual problem. Before Esther could muster up enough courage to express herself, he makes an attempt to fix the problem. Though this is a noble thing for the King to do it was not what she needed.

In reality, sometimes women accept material peace offering gifts from people who have harmed or hurt us. However, the gift is only a Band-Aid and does not fix the hurt, the betrayal, or even the thoughts about a hurt. We can accept gifts all day long and still be traumatized! Today, unfortunately we have a culture that promotes this toxic thinking as something that is normal. Media promotes the love scenario where the man buys a woman an elaborate gift and they ride off into the sunset as if everything was going to be great but it is not. If we buy into this type of fantasy it will set us up for failure every time. Hear me, something material will neither satisfy nor fix a nonmaterial problem. Please do not be fooled by the Hollywood films.

Instead, let's get to a point in our lives where we divorce the common knowledge of the world and take God at His word. From Esther, we see that she first prayed and fasted then she put on her royal garments, which were physical and spiritual, and stood in position silently. Even when she entered into the immediate presence of the King, she did so in silence and eventually had her wishes granted.

Chapter Eight
FINDING YOUR VOICE

"And the king said to Esther on the second day also as they drank their wine, "What is your petition, Queen Esther? It shall be granted to you. And what is your request? Even to half of the kingdom, it shall be done."

Esther 7:2

Esther is now in the presence of royalty unsummoned. She is in the defining moment of her embodiment of a woman of royal status and she has to proceed carefully. Though she has been equipped for this time, nothing compares to the day that destiny pulls your number. You can study for this moment, you can even dream about it, but what will you say when the microphone is in your hand? Will you stutter when asked to speak or will you muster the courage from deep within to speak with the liquidity of thought? It is time that you fully clock into purpose without the thought of returning to comfort.

A quick glance at the aforementioned scriptures above reveals that the King asked for Esther's need three times. King asks about her request and petition, which are two totally different questions. In English, the two words might seem synonymous with one another and we can use them in the absence of the other, but spiritually they carry very different weight. Request in the Hebrew comes from the word *bâqash* that means to search out, or to hold someone responsible for something because the speaker has legal right to. It also means to seek to secure the pursuit of a wish or accomplishing of a plan. Alternatively, petition comes from the Hebrew word *shâel*, which means to inquire, to demand, to beg and is also used for simple requests. Here, we see that the two words are constructed to ask two very different questions. What is the significance of the two questions? We receive the answers in Esther's response.

The Courageous Voice of Esther

After the third time the King sought after Esther's proposition, she revealed her purpose:

> *If I have found favor in your sight, O king, and if it pleases the king, let my life be spared as my petition, and my people [be spared] as my request.*

Esther petitions for her life and makes a request for the lives of her people. This is significant because a written decree was not made against her life specifically. In fact, the only known punishment stood for any person entering into the King's presence uninvited (Esther 4:11). Therefore, he could easily grant the petition for her life, which is a simple request (shâel). But, more needs to be done in order to fulfill the latter appeal because once a law is stamped by the King it cannot be reversed.

Haman, the identified enemy of the Jews approached the King in the first month of the twelfth year with news that the Jews did not obey the King's laws. He suggested that it would not be in the King's best interest that he continue to allow this behavior (Esther 3:8-9). Therefore, Haman proposed that he order their destruction and offered to foot the bill for their demise. Surprisingly, the King told Haman to keep the money and do as he pleased with the Jews as he signed the decree with his signet ring on the thirteenth day of the first month. Here, we see a quick turnaround in the decision concerning the lives of the Jews. Impulsively the King acted just as he had done with the issue concerning Vashti, which is also an action that he probably regretted. Yet, this time his decision affected thousands of people including Esther who had his favor.

The word *favor* in the Hebrew is *cheçed*, which means not only to have loyalty but also to have mercy. Since the common law was that anyone who enters into the King's presence uninvited would be killed, Esther took a great risk from the beginning. She reminds the King of the favor she once found with him when she replaced Vashti. What's telling here is that she relies on that favor once more before she exposes the desires of her heart. Ultimately, the meaning of *cheçed* is relevant in that it highlights the King's mercy that Esther is drawing upon. By the law, Esther deserved death because she went against the rules of the kingdom, but she obtained mercy. In the same way, God gives us grace by providing us with something we do not deserve, as well as mercy refraining from giving us something we do deserve.

The Favor in Destiny

> *"Favor is about position and occupying a platform."*
>
> Matthew Stevenson

In the beginning of the chapter, I drew your attention to three scriptures that highlighted the King's response to Esther's countenance. Three times Esther is offered a generous solution before she reveals her reason for being before him, and had three opportunities to throw in the towel and change her mind. She could have easily taken her chances on preserving her life and let the Jews fight for themselves, but she didn't abandon the opportunity to walk in her calling.

Granted, when destiny calls it will be a scary thing, and the enemy will offer you easier avenues on which to travel in order to deter you. However, the alternate routes will not sustain you and they will waste more of your time. Remember, the enemy is a consumer of time and he wants to keep you occupied until you have suspended all of your energies on a dead thing instead of the God thing. Perhaps, it might not be a dead thing, but a good thing; however, there is a difference between a good and God. Sister, the more time the enemy can steal from you the more he can prevent you from living on purpose. If you live outside of your purpose, it can potentially cause your life to stutter with the seduction of living beneath who God created you to be.

Looking back to the significance of the three times the King asked, the number three in the Bible represents completeness and perfection. In the Hebrew and in reference to this story the word for three is *shêber*, which means to breach. The word breach in this context can be interpreted multiple ways. It can illuminate a breach between Haman and the King. It can also signify a breach between Esther and her timid ways, as well as highlight a change in the King. Either way, the breach is significant in each instance and is in accordance to the destiny of the Jews. Furthermore, Esther fasted for three days and reveals her intent after the third question, which signals her ability to break strong barriers between God, herself, and the King.

Hence, we cannot deny God's favor in the story. If we dig further into the word favor it means that the stronger party remains committed to his promise, but retains his freedom especially with regard to the manner in which he will implement those promises. The definition continues to explain that the relationship, if sound, far transcends mere legalities. Now, I almost had a praise break when the Holy Spirit revealed this to me. In Esther, the "stronger party" is the King who holds all the power in the land. We will see that the King is very much committed to his promise to Haman because he signed it with his ring. However, he does implement an alternate decree that makes his former position null and void because he "retain[ed] his freedom" to do so. Ultimately, the relationship between he and Esther "far transcends mere legalities."

In essence, your destiny will be accompanied with favor! Thankfully, God will not call you to do something and not provide you a way of executing the plan. He is faithful and will never leave you in harm's way because there is a strategy for what he called you to do.

Strengthening of the Voice

"Esther said, "If it pleases the king, may the king and Haman come this day to the banquet that I have prepared for him."
Esther 5:4

"If I have found favor in the sight of the king, and if it pleases the king to grant my petition and to do as I request, may the king and Haman come to the banquet that I will prepare for them; and tomorrow I will do as the king says [and express my request]."
Esther 5:8

"Then Queen Esther replied, 'If I have found favor in your sight, O king, and if it pleases the king, let my life be spared as my petition, and my people [be spared] as my request;'"
Esther 7:3

Esther gave two responses to the King before she made her true intentions known. While it may seem that she is stalling, I contend that God is strengthening her even the more. Until Esther is granted permission by God to reveal her true intentions, she is silent on the matter. Therefore, the emphasis should not necessarily be on the banquet, but the act of preparation. The word prepare in the Hebrew comes from the words *âsâh* and *kûwn*. The former (âsâh) means to make something into something. In a theological sense, the word is used of man's response to divine commands and in his acts, he demonstrates his inward commitment to his relationship with God. According to the definition of the word, doing God's commands brings life upon a man, and *âsâh* can also be applied to all aspects of divine acts and actions. The latter explanation for *kûwn* means to be erect, established, readied, prepared, certain, and admissible. This root used concretely connotes being firm and unmoved, which lends itself to also being established in the sense of being ready.

God allowed the King to ask Esther three times about her petition and request because He was strengthening her ability to hear Him clearly. Granted, Esther fasted and turned to hear the voice of the Lord, but that does not mean that she fully understood what He wanted her to relay to the King. Esther's fast helped her come into a deeper awareness of who she was in Christ. Still, Esther needed further preparation as she needed to be readied for the assignment. While in the natural realm the second feast was hosted on the next day, time was escalated in the spirit. Remember, your obedience serves as a signal to God of growth, which allows Him to accelerate things for you.

Have you ever heard someone say that obedience is better than sacrifice? They are referring to 1 Samuel 15:22, but only quote the b-clause of the verse. The context of this scripture is such: God told the prophet Samuel to anoint King Saul to be King over Israel. The Lord gave Saul very strict instructions to destroy all the Amalekites and everything they had, including women, children, gold, silver, and animals. However, Saul decided to spare Agag, who was the King of the Amalekites and the best of his riches. When God revealed to the prophet Samuel that Saul did not fully obey His commandments, he sent Samuel back to Saul to confront him. When Saul saw Samuel, he lied and said that he carried out the orders of the Lord. Having revelation from God, Samuel exposed the deceit and told Saul that he would no longer be King.

Now, we might think that Saul did everything the Lord commanded except kill the leader and destroy some of the spoils. Yet, "everything" and "except" work in opposition to dually cancel one another. In obeying God halfway, Saul was in complete disobedience and was punished. 1 Samuel 15:23 tells us that "disobedience is as [serious as] false religion and idolatry." Saul rejected the word of the Lord in his half obedience and he was also rejected as King. Do you see how God views your disobedience? It is not just a little disobedience or you just dragging your feet. Ultimately, you are in direct opposition with the Lord and He takes it seriously. Your rebellion is on the same table as false religion and idolatry, which are very serious offenses to the Creator!

What if Esther would have taken the King's offer of half his kingdom? What would have come of her? Well, one possibility is that she would have been removed from her position as Queen just like Vashti. God would have probably raised up another woman to plead the case of the Jews to the King. Please hear me, you must understand that the Lord is no respecter of persons and you can be replaced. I know Beyoncé has that song Irreplaceable, but that's not true here. You are replaceable.

Esther could have also received the same punishment as Saul. When Samuel identified and anointed David as the next King of Israel the scripture says that the Spirit of the Lord departed from Saul, and an evil spirit from the Lord tormented and terrified (1 Samuel 16:14). Psychologically speaking, the evil spirit could be understood as mental illness. Saul thought he was losing his mind, and he became so obsessed with killing David that it consumed his entire life. But Esther saw what happened to Vashti as a result of disobedience to the authority in her life and she applied it to her spiritual authorities who were Mordecai and God.

God demonstrates the power of His timing before he gives Esther permission to make her request known through the final two tests. The fast strengthened Esther spiritually, the first feast demonstrated her inward commitment to God (âsâh), and the second feast established her in the sight of the King (kûwn).

How This Relates to You!

More times than not, the enemy uses the confines of your life against you. He magnifies your circumstances, past, and insecurities in order to get you to opt out of your destiny. While he cannot directly do anything to your destiny, he can get you to sabotage it by offering you different routes. Therefore, you should not flirt with the alternate routes because they will always lead you to discontentment in your spirit.

In Matthew 12:34, the Bible says that out of the abundance of the heart the mouth speaks, and what is in the heart eventually bleeds over into our personality. We then begin to speak what is lodged deep within. Unfortunately, before we realize the damage that we have incurred over time, it mixes with our personality so seamlessly that we don't realize that we have an issue. But it's not too late to change. The enemy wants you to stay married to the spirit of stuck. He wants you to be immovable without vision and okay with the status quo. However, God has something better for you!

In my journey of self-awareness, I've learned the importance of not settling even if there are no potential prospects in my life. I had to learn the hard consequences of being disobedient.

Honestly, it has been a tough time for me to unlearn the things that I picked up along the way by associating with people on those alternative routes. I unknowingly ascribed to their beliefs, habits, and mindsets no matter how ugly. Due to my disobedience, God had to refine me and it hurt badly.

Unfortunately, a lot of times, as women, we play the blame game. He hurt me. She gossiped about me. My dad wasn't there. No one helped me, but what happens to the responsibility that we take in our own lives? When do we have permission to admit that we dropped the ball on ourselves, and agreed to the toxic behavior that we learned? What if Esther did not adhere to the promptings of God? What if she decided that this was time that she cared for herself when others didn't value women? If she'd succumbed to any of those thoughts, a whole race of people would have been massacred. Therefore, it is crucially important that we align ourselves with the work of the Lord and that we stand firm in what he tells us to do even if no one around us cosigns on the assignment.

Lady, I want you to understand that your purpose and destiny are tied to the lives of so many other people. It is in your obedience that they will get saved and you will remain sane. It is in your sacrifice that you will help them not in your selfishness. Your brokenness is for a reason! Your pain and your sensitivity is all for the glory of God. There are people are waiting for you who crave and will crave the gift of who you are. Therefore, every decision that you make or don't make has a consequence. While we love the good consequences that we call blessings, we dislike the negative repercussions and we try to make excuses like Saul. When he is found out he tells Samuel,

I have sinned; for I have transgressed the commandment of the Lord and [Samuel's] words, because I feared the people and obeyed their voice." (1 Samuel 15:24)

Please do not think that you will escape the reaping of your actions, and that God will excuse you from what He told you to do. Just because you may be afraid that people will be mean and talk about you, it doesn't excuse you from your calling. Other people's opinions do not matter to God, and you have to be delivered from people pleasing because it equates to self-deprivation. This was a sobering reality for me when I realized that people could potentially perish because of my disobedience. So, I encourage you not to allow the opinions of others to cripple and deter you from moving in the direction that God has set for you.

Chapter Nine

QUEENLY ACTIONS

"For we have been sold, I and my people, to be destroyed, killed and wiped out of existence. Now if we had only been sold as slaves, men and women, I would have remained silent, for our hardship would not be sufficient to burden the king [by even mentioning it]."

Esther 7:4

Y ou will need to develop a complete trust in God to perform confidently Queenly actions. Your total reliance on Him will yield you the courage you need to sustain you. At this point, Esther has the ability to showcase confidence when she addresses the King boldly in Esther 7:4. She stood before him without coaching or even visible fear. In a powerful way, she embraced and dominated her calling.

This chapter will address the charge of Women of Royalty. While we know that Esther's calling is bigger than herself, we have yet to explore just how big it is. Yes, her actions impacted all the Jews, but what does that mean for her as a woman? I think it is important to pay attention to her in this phase of her life because the woman who she becomes is a testament to God's commitment to us. God delights in women so much that He partners with us to bring forth children in the earth. He trusts us to bear His thoughts in the womb of our body and that is not something that should be taken lightly. However, there are a couple more characteristics that deserve attention in Esther's embodiment as Queen before we get there.

Shortly we will see the enemy of the Jews beg and almost flee for his life after Esther exposes his evil plot. Because Esther completely trusted in the power of God and leaned not on her own understanding, she had the ability to take a powerful stance before the King.

She drew attention to the fact that her people, the Jews, were treated horribly. In fact, they were destroyed, killed, and wiped out of existence. The King James version says that the Jews were destroyed, killed, and annihilated. Now, in American culture we might use these words interchangeably, as with others, without much thought of their significance. But, each word, carries a weight of its own like all the other words that I have explicated thus far. According to the Miriam-Webster dictionary the words destroy, kill, and annihilate means to cause destruction or damage to something so boldly that it can't be repaired; to end the life of something; and to cause to be of no effect, respectively. From these three definitions we have the ability to see that there are varying degrees of negative trauma that can occur, and the Jews have withstood them all.

While God uses Esther as a representative to save the lives of the Jews, she won a major battle with the King in secret. Remember, when she went before him unsummoned and should have been killed? It was her courage that gave her strength and God's favor that allowed her to come out unharmed. In Esther 7:4, Esther says that if the Jews were to be sold as slaves then she wouldn't bring the matter to the King's attention, but she cannot sit idly by since there is a new threat of mass extermination. The cause is the most beautiful realization in this chapter. Esther, who is culturally linked to the Jews by birth uses her positioning to fight on their behalf. Generally, we think of culture in terms of birth and that is correct, but you can also be culturally linked to people based on dysfunction, school, trauma, and church because culture is an expression of being in a collective identity.

One major step in taking royal actions is realizing that there is a reason that you are alive. You have a purpose whether you believe it or not and your pain serves as the sounding board to set someone's life in order. While you might not understand it, you have to believe that you were built for the struggle of your life and that God will never leave you nor forsake you!

I reflect back on when God challenged me to write this book and the struggle I had with admitting that I didn't have a firm grasp my identity. I didn't want to admit that I once hid behind my degrees because I didn't really love myself. However, I realized that in order to write this book I would have to be honest not only with myself but with the whole world. Coming into the knowledge of the truth through writing has freed me enough to allow me to share with you. As I write, I consistently reflect on those moments where I thought that there was no hope for me because I'd never seen anyone be free until later in their life. Yet, the Holy Spirit told me that there were people waiting for me. He reminded me that there were women who were looking for someone like me to be the model that highlights that living for Jesus is worth it. Therefore, I write in expectation that you will come into the truth of your identity. I write because there is a cause.

Expose the Hidden Things

"Esther said, "An adversary and an enemy is Haman, this evil man." Then Haman became terrified before the king and queen."

Esther 7:6

The enemy would love nothing more than to keep you bound to your past. In fact, it would make his day if you are still attempting to cope with those things that happened to you. Perhaps it's that relationship that did not work out, or the fact that one of your parents was not around. He uses all of your past hang ups to his advantage until he can fully destroy your life. Not only will he torment you by reminding you of the things that did not work out, but he will encourage you to torment yourself by coxing you into rehearsing past experiences. If you are not careful you will become a victim to the very thing you want freedom from and it will make you miserable. I can attest to this truth and it was not until I allowed people to call me out on my actions, until I allowed God to prune me, until I fell out of agreement with my past that I became free.

In the same manner, the first step in freeing the Jews was to expose the enemy Haman. Esther does not just identify Haman as the perpetrator, but she identifies him as he is, an "adversary and enemy." Of course she could have just identified him as an enemy, but she does not stop there. She also calls him an adversary. I love that the New Revised Standard Version (NRSV) of the verse identifies Haman as a foe, enemy, and wicked man. In order to find the significance of her speech, and the importance of the three adjectives, we have to delve into their meanings. The word foe comes from the Hebrew word *sânê*, which connotes an emotion ranging from intense hatred to jealousy, and also signifies being set against something. On the other hand, the word enemy comes from the Greek word *ôwyêb*, which is used in reference to individuals, nations, and personal foes.

I want to break this down further so that you can catch the weight of Esther's revelation. When the King promoted Haman and Mordecai refused to bow to him, Haman was a personal foe of Mordecai:

All the king's servants who were at the king's gate [in royal service] bowed down and honored and paid homage to Haman; for this is what the king had commanded in regard to him. But Mordecai [a Jew of the tribe of Benjamin] neither bowed down nor paid homage [to him]. (Esther 3:3)

The Bible says that,

"When Haman saw that Mordecai neither bowed down nor paid homage to him, he was furious" (Esther 3:5)."

To Haman, Mordecai was blatantly disrespectful and if his behavior was tolerated then he could possibly encourage others to be disobedient. Remember also how the sages felt about Vashti's disobedience, which is in correlation to Haman's feelings for Mordecai.

More importantly, the tensions between Haman and the Jews go back further than Mordecai's refusal to bow. If you remember chapter 2, I mentioned the lineage through which Esther descended. She came from the tribe of Benjamin and therefore was a Benjamite. Haman, on the other hand, is an Agagite who descends from the Amalekite lineage. He is a descendant of King Agag who was an Amalekite, and the Amalekites were the first people to launch unwarranted attacks against Israel. Anyone who has ever attacked or even attempted to attack the children of Israel saw great demise.

As a result of the Amalekites' actions, the Lord decreed their extinction. If you remember, I told you about Saul's disobedience to God when He told him to destroy all the Amalekites. King Saul spared Agag, and therefore, Saul's kingship was taken from him and given to David. Well, let's just say that if Saul had killed Agag then we would not have to worry about Haman because he would not exist. Yet, due to Saul's disobedience the enemy of the children of Israel was made flesh. I think it is safe to say that your actions now will continue to follow your lineage and the rest of the people of the world long after you have expired.

Nodding back to Esther, both foe and enemy are great ways to describe Haman because he was a personal foe of Mordecai who would not bow, and was an enemy of the children of Israel because of God's favor on them. The Bible also shows that Haman wanted revenge:

He disdained laying hands on Mordecai alone, for they had told him who the people of Mordecai were (his nationality); so Haman determined to destroy all the Jews, the people of Mordecai, who lived throughout the kingdom of Ahasuerus. (Esther 3:6)

So, when he went before the King and accused all of the Jews of being a hazard to the kingdom he says:

> Then Haman said to King Ahasuerus, 'There is a certain people scattered [abroad] and dispersed among the peoples in all the provinces of your kingdom; their laws are different from those of all other people, and they do not observe the king's laws. Therefore, it is not in the king's interest to [tolerate them and] let them stay here. (Esther 3:8)

In essence, Mordecai's refusal was added fuel to an already simmering fire. I am sure Haman knew that majority of his people were destroyed because of the war with Israel. I also imagine that he set his heart to avenge them by inciting that all the Jews be destroyed like his people. Mordecai, then, was a constant reminder of the irritation of Haman with the Jews. Now that he had power he could do something about the chosen people of God, or so he thought!

Esther also called Haman an evil man but the NRSV calls him a wicked man. This might seem like common knowledge because we know what he planned for the Jews; but, it holds a bit more significance than our mere observations. In the Hebrew, the word for wicked is *ra* and it connotes a breach of harmony and the ability to break up what is good and desirable for man and society. The explication links back to our previous discussion about breaches, and goes farther to suggest that one of the most marked features of the ungodly man is the injury that his actions causes others around him.

Haman's actions were not only destructive to the Jews, but they could've brought shame on the King, and his horrible behavior backfired on him. When Esther exposed him and his plot to the King, he was hung on the very gallows that he planned for Mordecai (Esther 7:9). Even more, his ten sons were killed because they were his descendants (Esther 9:7). Hence, Esther exposed Haman and did not spare his life or his descendants' lives. Lady, you will have to identify the enemy when you allow God to come into your life and rebuild you. The Holy Spirit will begin to show you the enemies of your lineage and of your personal life. God will also reveal to you the plans of the enemy for your life. Remember, the devil wants to encourage you to become another statistic to shut your mouth, and the generational curses that run through your family do not want to stop with you, but also wants to consume your descendants. Thankfully, when you submit your will to Christ, he will start to show you how to fight against the generational curses and reroute the enemy's plans for you. The Lord may also begin to show you how you became a willing participant in the plans of the enemy. If I can be honest, there are periods when we are openly disobedient and ignore the promptings of God. In doing so, we unknowingly side with the devil in our own demise. Yes, we have a familial enemy, but our personal foes are specifically catered to our lives and it surfaces in many ways.

However, women have been exposers of the enemy since the days of Adam and Eve. It was Eve who identified the serpent as the perpetrator of deception and after she exposed the serpent God cursed him. So take courage in knowing that God will help you.

Persistence and Focus

"Then Esther spoke again to the king and fell down at his feet and wept and implored him to avert the evil plot of Haman the

Agagite and his plan which he had devised against the Jews [because the decree to annihilate the Jews was still in effect]. Then the king held out to Esther the golden scepter. So Esther arose and stood before the king. Then she said, 'If it pleases the king and if I have found favor before him and the matter is proper in the king's view and I am pleasing in his sight, let it be written to revoke the letters devised by Haman the son of Hammedatha, the Agagite, which he wrote [in order] to destroy the Jews who are in all the king's provinces. For how can I endure to see the tragedy that will happen to my people? Or how can I endure to see the destruction of my kindred?'"

Esther 8:3-6

Esther could have rejoiced when the King ordered the execution of Haman, but her job was not done. His work was still at play though he and his sons were gone. We can also think of this in terms of soul ties. I do not want to assume that you are familiar with such a thing so I'll give you the short version. When you are intimate with someone, create memories with them, or even are just close friends you create soul ties. All soul ties are not sexual, but they are binding in a lot of ways. Imagine, if you will, the feeling one has when they breakup with a longtime lover. For some it feels like a divorce and for others it feels like death. The slow pain of the parting lasts longer than the conversation to leave one another. The agony people may feel signals that there is a soul tie. Perhaps the person consumes their thoughts, and emotions, and they find themselves in a can't eat, can't sleep mode. These are all clues of an active soul tie and the time spent with the other person created knots in their heart and spirit that holds the two together longer than wished. Therefore, it takes time to undo those knots because the essence of who that individual was in another's life lingers on, just like the actions of Haman were still visible after his death.

Sometimes we do not realize the consequences of the actions we make and do not make. There are tremors that are sent throughout the earth based on our positioning, or the lack thereof, and the decision to miss an opportunity impacts the entire universe. Esther realized this truth because she was still pleading with the King after Haman died. The first time she pleaded with him she asked that she and the Jews' lives be spared and he obliged. Now, she has to ask that consequences of the deal made with Haman be revoked. She wants the King to annul the decree, and in doing so she reveals that she is kin to the Jews. In the scripture, she finally calls them her family and that is powerful! When God puts a demand on our lives it will most likely be in the area of kinship. Esther was culturally kin to the Jews and her ability to identify with them caused her to be persistent. She could not just stop because Haman was gone, but she had to deal with the ramifications of his presence, which is something she probably would not have had to do if Saul would have obeyed God and destroyed Agag.

But, God sent a woman to finish what he previously commanded in the book of 1 Samuel. He sent someone who would submit to His instruction, though was perceived as weak and insignificant. He sent someone who he could trust. He sent Esther.

Sister, there is so much in this world that is distracting to our assignment. I want you to remember that one day this place will fade away and you will be gone. Personally, I never wanted God to tell me that I did not live up to the person He created me to be. I do not want the video reel to play in heaven of everything I could have had, but disqualified myself for. Over time, I've learned that I have to be careful about the things that I allow to steal my focus. Even things that may seem good may not be God ordained. I encourage you to humble yourself before the feet of the Lord and seek guidance on the pressing things, and your focus will flow out of this.

Rule and Responsibility

"Now she sent word and summoned Barak the son of Abinoam from Kedesh-naphtali, and said to him, "Behold, the Lord, the God of Israel, has commanded, 'Go and march to Mount Tabor, and take with you ten thousand men [of war] from the tribes of Naphtali and Zebulun. I will draw out Sisera, the commander of Jabin's army, with his chariots and his infantry to meet you at the river Kishon, and I will hand him over to you.'" Then Barak said to her, "If you will go with me, then I will go; but if you will not go with me, I will not go." She said, "I will certainly go with you; nevertheless, the journey that you are about to take will not be for your honor and glory, because the Lord will sell Sisera into the hand of a woman.' Then Deborah got up and went with Barak to Kedesh."

Judges 4:6-9

Esther is not the first woman in the Bible who had to make a tough decision. In the same way that Eve exposed the serpent, Deborah exposed the plan of God and prophesied to Barak in Judges. I encourage you to take a look at the Deborah's story for a more detailed understanding of her importance in the earth. For context here, Deborah was a prophetess, wife, agitator, warrior, poet, maternal figure, and judge of Israel. In *The Deborah Anointing*, Michelle McClain-Waters explains that,

The days of the Judges lasted between three and four hundred years...It was a season of moral outrage, a period of gross immorality, lawlessness, and violence...This resulted in a tragic compromising, permissive lifestyle of destruction and chaos.

Judges during that time were equivalent to the President today. They posed as deliverers, saviors, and liberators of oppressed people, and Deborah was a judge for twenty years. I mention Deborah because she has similar characteristics to Esther.

Deborah had the courage to go to war through her ability to hear from God. Like Esther, she did not back down from her assignment, and was strong in speech. Deborah was a woman of wisdom and operated in astuteness with her people just as Esther did with the King. She was a woman of prestige and Esther is a Woman of Royalty. By making these connections it is easier to understand the responsibility of the decisions that Esther makes in the final scriptures.

After the King signed a new law that voided his agreement with Haman, the Jews had the upper hand. The new ruling stated that the Jews had the permission to kill, destroy, and annihilate anyone who came against them, their children, and their belongings. The Jews, then, mobilized and others began to fear them because of their new willed power. The scripture highlights that even the people in the royal court were fearful of the Jews and their God (Esther 9).

Imagine how they felt to know that their lives were not only being spared, but they could defend themselves against anyone who came for them. The Bible tells us that they killed 75,000 men but didn't take their possessions. I believe that their ability to not take their enemy's belongings is significant because it was a previous command of God when Saul half obeyed in killing the Amalekites. Not only did God tell Saul to kill everyone but he also told him to destroy their belongings; therefore, he sent Esther ensure that His original plan was executed so that they will no longer be at risk of retaliation.

After the King gave the Jews permission to defend themselves, and after they killed the first 500 men, the King returns to Esther with two questions. He says,

> *The Jews have killed and destroyed five hundred men and the ten sons of Haman at the citadel in Susa. What then have they done in the rest of the king's provinces! Now what is your petition? It shall be granted to you. What is your further request? It shall also be done. (Esther 9:12)*

This is the third time the King has asked Esther about her petition and her request. Though previously she asked that her life and the lives of her people be spared, this time she shifts in her response.

> *"'If it pleases the king,' Esther answered, 'let it be granted to the Jews who are in Susa to act tomorrow also in accordance with the decree of today; and let [the dead bodies of] Haman's ten sons be hanged on the gallows'. (Esther 9:13)*

Her personal petition was to allow the Jews to fight again the next day. Esther wanted to ensure that the Jews were free of their enemies because if their enemies were destroyed then they wouldn't have to worry about backlash. Now, however, her request was for the sons of Haman to be hung. The request is crucial because it allegorizes the intent of God. Since the sons of Haman were already deceased why would Esther order their lifeless bodies to be suspended?

Let's think about this request in the context of a suicide. When one commits suicide by hanging, the material used around the neck cuts off the air supply to the body forging a separation of the oxygen from the lungs to the brain (i.e. from the chest to the head). The suffocating material is used to sever the flow of oxygen. In the same vein, by hanging the dead bodies, Esther symbolically suffocates the legacy and impact of the Amalekites through hanging Haman's sons. Because the head speaks to leadership and government, allegorizing the dislocation of the head from the body signals a shift in authoritative powers. The hanging bodies also serve as visual warning for anyone who thinks of attacking the Jews in the future.

Lady, I'm sure you know this by now, but I want to reiterate: When God calls you to do something it will be hard. If it is not bigger than you, if it does not frighten you in some way, then it probably is not from God. You might not understand why he requires certain things from you, and I get it, but you have to trust in His plan. If you obey what He has called you to do, if you say what He has told you to say, if you follow the path He has designed for you then you will have the victory.

Chapter Ten

ROYALTY UNMASKED

"Then Queen Esther, the daughter of Abihail, with Mordecai the Jew, wrote with full power and authority to confirm this second letter about Purim."

Esther 10:29

The book of Esther ends in triumph for the Jews. Haman and his sons are destroyed and the Jews gain power over everyone who sought to kill them. On the day that they were to be originally executed they stood before their enemies and had the victory. Not only were the commoners in fear, but the officials, chief rulers, governors, and anyone else who attended to the King's business were as well. We see that God really showed up for the Jews because they followed His commands and trusted in His promises.

Their victory was commemorated by the Feast of Purim. The reason that the feast is important is two-fold: The Jews wanted to celebrate annually their victory over their enemies, and Haman cast Pur (lots) to find the best time to ask for their destruction (Esther 9:24). The duality of the significance of the date highlights the power and hand of God in the story. God turned the situation around for their good through their intentional prayer, fasting, and faithfulness.

And for Esther, she embodied the royal status that was ordained for her. In moving from an orphan who was largely insecure and rejected to a Woman of Royalty, we have the opportunity to glean nuggets of wisdom from her life's charge. Throughout the journey, Esther demonstrated an obedient spirit because she realized that she could not afford to lean on her own understanding. In the end, she wrote with full power and authority, which signals that she came into alignment with the position that God had for her.

The Inner Me Enemy

After Esther completed her commitment to the Jews, the Bible references the name of her father again. I wondered why we were reminded of him at this point. God revealed to me that He is showing us that just because we go from glory to glory, or faith to faith does not mean that we will not have to deal with the other enemies of our past. In essence, we do not know the full extent of things that were operative in Esther's life that were in opposition to the will of God. We do not know if she still silently struggled with being an orphan or not. This possibility highlights that we will always need God even after we win a battle.

In all honestly, we need Him more after our victories because often the fight is so great that we are left weakened in some area. In our moments of retreat, the enemy will continuously remind us of where we came from and why we are not good enough. He will bring up something from our past that God has already forgiven us for, so that he can build kingdoms of defeat in our minds. Yes, Esther exposed Haman. Yes, she liberated the Jews. Yes, she saved the King's life, but she still was the daughter of Abihail. She still had a history and she still struggled with things behind closed doors.

Sometimes we allow people to get drunk on the highlight reel of our lives without showing the areas in which we still bleed. We can get so happy that we are moving in purpose to the point that we start running from the memories of yesterday. In spite of the power and authority that Esther gained in the end of her quest, she was still a woman who had not fully tended to her private pains. Even after the beautification process, there were still traces of past hopes, dreams, and trauma that remained. She was beautiful enough to go forward, but not healed enough to not need the Lord. An understanding of your purpose is the first step of understanding your identity, and it will give you momentum when you want to stop. It will also help you see things from a heavenly perspective instead of a carnal one, but it will not immediately heal every broken part of you.

The Work of Identity

As you operate in purpose there will be times when God uncovers another level of brokenness from your past. Generally, people believe they are healed from something until someone gets close enough to push against the wound exposing its soreness. Yes, there is a scar there but underneath the scab the flesh is still tender because there is still a need for healing underneath the surface. This is how operating in purpose that leads to identity awareness works. The more you press into it and into God, the more you will become healed. Sometimes you will receive healing in areas that you didn't know where fractured, and other times the healing will be obvious.

For Esther, while God called the woman into purpose, he still had to deal with the girl inside of her. Inside of every woman there is a young girl waiting to be healed, and inside of every young girl there is a woman who hopes to emerge in destiny. What are you teaching your young girl on the inside of you? The girl who suffers from abandonment, daddy issues, or low self-esteem? How are you soothing her pain as she fights to become better than she was treated?

We see that Esther still had an appointment with God because of her unhealed parental area. The call on Esther's life demanded that she move in spite of being hurt. She did not have time to take inventory of her pain because she had to worry about everyone else. Women are really guilty of this. We keep moving without paying attention to the silent screams of our soul begging us to stop and heal. We push past the hurt and hope that no one finds out that we still struggle with things that happened to us in childhood. We mask the essence of who we are for the praise of others until the thing we have tried to outrun catches up with us. Esther's hang-up was the lack of relationship with her father who was her protector, but what is yours? What is that thing that causes you to shut down when it is mentioned? That thing you still cry about at night in the comfort of your room? The thing you've pushed down for so many years that when you even think someone will ask you about it you get an attitude? Yes, that thing. That thing that torments you at night and causes you to believe that everyone else got something that you did not. That thing that seduces you to hold on to it even if it hurts.

Lady, please here me: God will allow the areas of undealt with pain to catch up to you. He will allow you to move past all the obstacles until your time of confrontation because if you do not deal with that unconfronted area then it will hinder you in the next phase of destiny. Your willingness to move in your purpose is admirable, but your tending to your inner needs is beautiful.

Personally, I thought that I successfully moved past certain areas in my life when I finished this book a year prior. I thought that because I finally understood my purpose and was moving into alignment with God that I was free of all the things in my past. It was shocking for me to discover that I still struggled in some hidden places even after fulfilling the charge on my life. It was after a yearlong process—my own beautification process—that remnants of my past started to chase after me. It was after I finished fighting the greatest battle of my life that I noticed old habits and proclivities starting to resurface. I thought that I dealt with them, but I only put them on the backburner in an attempt to fulfill my purpose. So when my old hurts started to bubble up into my present, I had to stop and deal with them. If I can be honest, it was tough for me to go back and tend to those old wounds because I thought that if I functioned at high capacity then no one would notice that I was still hurting. I reasoned that if I moved fast enough then I would be able to outmaneuver those things that threatened my destiny, but I was wrong. I have learned that in this battle called life there will always be something after your progress and it will not stop until you wage war with it.

The Call to W.O.R

The enemy will fight you on this charge and I must start off by telling you this. He wants you to be bound for your entire time on earth so that you and those connected to you cannot live freely. He wants you to be depressed, heartbroken, and bitter so that he can accomplish His plans in the earth, but it is time that we wage wor. The spelling of wor is not a typo but it is an intentional reference to the type of woman you will become. By becoming a Woman of Royalty, you actively engage in the art of war with the enemy and his camp. You become a weapon in the hands of God to beat down the enemy and cause great demise to hell. You are a bad mamma jamma. You are a warrior. In this battle, you are the victor. You have completed the prerequisites and basic training needed to enlist in God's army. You are now cleared to stand firmly on the battle field with the armor of God to effectively track, trace, and demolish any satanic attempt at your life or the lives of the people to who you are called.

Women of Royalty do not just sit on thrones and look pretty; they are skillful, intelligent people. They are in the homes and the boardrooms. They are teachers and counselors. They are history makers and world changers. Women of Royalty are strategically placed throughout the earth to affect change. We are the carriers of life and each day we have the opportunity to have a Genesis moment. We are the gatekeepers of the palace and we hold power when we work with God.

Unmasking Your Royalty

I want you to make a commitment to yourself to remove your mask. I want you to challenge yourself to become better, love better, and live better. I hope that my transparency has helped and encouraged you to embark upon your own journey towards royalty. I know that it can be a scary thing because you do not know what the new you has in store, but think about the possibility of being a fragment of who you were designed to be. There are several factors that contribute to your personal journey and the things you learn along the way will shape your outcome. However, the beautiful places are not necessarily on the other side of the wilderness, but in the person you become as you move forward. I do not want to sell you a dream and lead you to believe that this thing will be pretty because it will not, but it will be worth it. So, if you are ready to realize fully your place of royalty, pray this prayer and let's get to work!

> *Father,*
> *I admit that I have lived a life lower than that You have called me to. I admit that I have taken things into my own hands for a long time, but now I am ready to surrender them to You. You know my areas of weakness and my areas of strength. You knit me together in my mother's womb and I praise You. God, I ask that You lead me on the personal path of realizing my arena of royalty. I am the daughter of the Most High King and as I come into the knowledge of who I am, I ask that You release to me my inheritance. Make me beautiful again, Dad. Make me prestigious. Make me a Queen! In Jesus' name I pray, Amen.*

Welcome to your Palace! Your throne awaits!

REFERENCES

John Bevere, The Bait of Satan: Living Free from the Deadly Trap of Offense (Charisma House, 2004) 7.

Michelle McClain-Waters, The Esther Anointing (Charisma House, 2014), 36.

Michelle McClain-Waters, The Deborah Anointing (Charisma House, 2015), 20.

ACKNOWLEDGEMENTS

There are so many people who made this book possible and I cannot thank them all here; but please know that I am grateful for your contributions, encouraging words, and belief in me as a woman. I'd like to thank my parents, who both contributed to my life and thoughts in their own special ways. Thanks to my friends Allison, Ashley, Kendria, and Khirsten for pushing me when I wanted to stop. Thanks to Cindy who encouraged me to walk in my truth.

I am also thankful for the various men and women in the body of Christ who have paved the way to make this book possible. Without your obedience to God, I may not have made it to this point as quickly as I have.

Lastly, thank you to all my readers. I am grateful for you! I pray that you will find truth in the pages of this book that will encourage you to live as the Queen that God created.

ABOUT THE AUTHOR

Dr. Briana Whiteside is native of Chicago, Illinois. As a Christian-Academic, she believes in the importance of the longstanding relationship between the secular and the sacred and uses this understanding in her teachings. She is commit-ted to helping women discover their identity in Christ and live a life of freedom. Her three aca-demic degrees coupled with the power of the Holy Spirit allows her to reach a wide range of women who may not fit into specific category designations.

STAY CONNECTED

Thank you for purchasing Woman of Royalty. Briana would like to connect with you. Below are a few ways you can connect with Briana, stay posted on events, get updates on new releases, and more!

FACEBOOK Briana Whiteside
WEBSITE www.brianawhiteside.com
INSTAGRAM Briana Whiteside
EMAIL briana@brianawhiteside.com

30050573R00088

Made in the USA
Middletown, DE
23 December 2018